Aces of the Air

9

BYRD

SOUTH POLE FLIGHT

From the sphere of storm and cold,
Death and night—the ice king's hold,
Comes one back in hero's mold,—
    Byrd!

Vikings, tired of storm and sea,
Franklin, Nansen, Peary, ye!
But, O child of destiny,—
    Byrd!

          —Joseph Lewis French

Captain Eddie Rickenbacker, U.S.A.

America's Ace of Aces

France, 1918

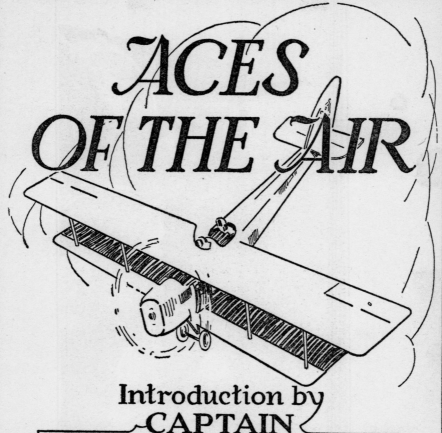

ACES OF THE AIR

Introduction by CAPTAIN EDDIE RICKENBACKER

Edited by
JOSEPH LEWIS FRENCH

McLOUGHLIN BROS. INC.
SPRINGFIELD, MASS.

This Book was Designed, Printed and Bound
in SPRINGFIELD, MASSACHUSETTS
U.S.A.

FOREWORD

IT was with pleasure I learned that our old friend, Joseph Lewis French, was preparing another book on Aviation and its development.

Aviation is only in its infancy, and as we are standing on the threshold of a tremendous growth in this line, we all realize there is yet much to be accomplished from both a scientific and manufacturing standpoint.

However, Aviation is destined to become, in the not too distant future, what the automotive industry is to the world today.

The boys of today will be the men of tomorrow. They will be the ones who will be guiding the destinies of our country.

Not only will they be Aviation pilots and mechanics, as they may now dream of, but many will become the financial and commercial leaders in the large enterprises of this great industry.

Many may have the good fortune to become Good Will envoys such as Lindbergh; others may use Aviation as a means of transportation for exploring the Great Unknown, as Commander Byrd is doing today, or follow in the footsteps of such world renowned engineers and designers as the Wright Brothers, Anthony Fokker and numerous others, to whom we extend our heartfelt thanks for making Aviation the fundamental success it is today.

There is, therefore, an opportunity for every boy who has the privilege of reading this book, or the desire to become associated with Aviation, to decide just what phase of the business he wishes to enter and prepare himself accordingly.

11

I am glad to note the tremendous interest in Aviation that is being displayed by our boys today, and to the American Youth, who choose Aviation as their life work, may I extend my sincerest wishes for their every success, and trust they will prepare themselves to continue the development of this great science for which our pioneers and Aviation leaders have laid such a firm foundation.

New York City
November 1, 1929

CONTENTS

13

14 CONTENTS

MY FLIGHT TO 39,140 FEET

BY LIEUT. APOLLO SOUCEK, U. S. N.
Holder of the World's Altitude Record

TODAY (May 8) is the day we have been waiting for for more than a week. The sky is clear of clouds, the air cool, the sun brilliant.

My Wright Apache plane is on the line, the mechanics are giving it the last touches—forty gallons of gas in the tanks, which must lift me higher than man has ever flown before. Captain Luke Christopher, chairman of the contest committee of the National Aeronautic Association, with the aid of Chief Electrician's Mate Fagan, is sealing the barographs and placing them in the compartment next to my oxygen bottles.

I am almost stifled in my heavy flying suit, boots and mittens, while Commander F. H. Sears, flight surgeon of the Naval Air Station, plugs my nostrils to force me to breathe through the mouth; adjusts my goggles, with their six pin holes through which I must see when the glasses eventually become covered with frost, coats them in attempts to slow down the frost formation and adjusts my helmet and face mask.

Chief Machinist Mates Enricksen and Kidder, who have nursed my plane for weeks in preparation for today's venture, give the engine a last test.

15

Mechanics cling to the tiny plane to hold it down as I race the motor. Everything is ready. The day is perfect. We ought to do it today if at all. I taxi the plane out into the field.

The take-off is easy, after a run of 25 yards. I slip my goggles over my forehead to prevent the collection of moisture until I need them and head out over the Potomac. We're off.

My left eye begins to pain, a grain of sand driven into it as we took off, which may cause trouble. It is uncomfortable breathing through my mouth as the plane, stepped at an angle of thirty degrees, climbs rapidly—3,000 feet a minute for the first few minutes.

It's a long way up, so I throttle the motor down slightly to save it for the big pull at the top.

I had determined to make the climb in ever-widening circles, with the naval air station, my home field, at the center. The first 10,000 feet is easy—in about four minutes.

The atmosphere is as clear as crystal. Off to the north I can see Baltimore clearly. To the west is the smoke fringe of the Blue Ridge Mountains.

But that was just a glance over the side. My eyes belong on the instruments in the cockpit. They need more eyes and hands than I have.

Now we are at 12,000 feet. Time to turn on the oxygen, ever so slightly; not that I need it now, but Dr. Sears says it is best. I want to conserve all my strength for the long pull up above. I can do this by using the oxygen at the earlier stages of the flight where the air still has enough oxygen to sustain life.

By this time the ever-widening circles of my flight are fifteen miles in diameter.

Now we are up to 15,000 feet. A strong southwest wind at this altitude, fully seventy miles an hour. Too strong to permit me to maintain the circles I had planned. The wind is blowing as fast as the plane up in this level.

The best thing to do is to stick my nose up into the wind and let both the wind and the motor lift us. So we climb up into the wind, staying over the same spot, apparently right over the Arlington Memorial.

We are climbing now at a little steeper angle. I pull back the stick to get up faster.

The air speed indicator says we are traveling at 75 miles an hour. I am supposed to slow down the speed one mile for each 1,000 feet of climb. We will be going just as fast, but the air, as it grows rarer, flowing through the venture tube to the air speed indicator, does not actuate the indicator as much as down on the ground. The rate of climb is probably falling off, but I guess we are getting better than 2,000 feet a minute even now.

My radius of vision begins to increase. The clear day enables me to see a horizon now 50 miles away. Now we are at 20,000 feet. I begin to feel the cold air around my eyes.

The temperature is falling rapidly, so I put on my goggles to prevent the possibility of freezing my eyes and eyelids. The plane keeps its steady climb into the wind, on up to 30,000 feet. The appearance of the earth below is much the same as at 20,000 feet.

Now we are getting up into it. From now on things will go harder. The engine begins to show signs of needing more air. The dial which shows engine revolutions drops from the normal 2,000 revolutions a minute to 1,700. We can't go much higher without more air in the engine. The air is too rare.

Time to close the supercharger valve, deflecting the air into the carburetor, reproducing the conditions on the ground. The Wasp picks up at once, the engine revolutions go back to normal. The old ship is climbing again at a better rate, but still much slower than down below.

All this time I have been opening the oxygen valves wider and wider. Breathing becomes more difficult. I am feeling a little bit weak and very tired, as if I had not slept for days. That's the signal again—I need more oxygen.

Time, too, to supercharge the gas tank. The gas pressure is getting low. I need that gas in the engine. Still we climb. Now we are at 37,000 feet, where the trouble begins. Though we are headed westward and making probably sixty miles an hour, the wind is too strong for us. It is carrying us backwards, slowly. At this same speed we would be making ninety miles an hour on the ground.

I don't feel the cold, but I realize that it is getting very cold. My shoulder is tired from the strain of pushing on the supercharger valve. I try to turn to keep the bend in the Potomac at Washington in view, but it is hard work. The light oil which lubricates the controls—the ailerons, elevator and rudder,—has frozen, and it is all I can do to move that stick.

Now comes the tough part. Now the battle will begin in earnest. However, everything has gone so successfully thus far, I have visions of climbing to at least 42,000 feet on my altimeter. It looks within my grasp. I had better look around. From now on I'll be too busy to look out again. I need my bearings, too. I can still see the Potomac's bend at Washington, but the naval air station has disappeared.

The capital is a blur on the ground too small to permit me to distinguish buildings. I can see the fine, parallel lines of streets. Hains Point stands out like a tiny pickle.

North of me I can see the head of Chesapeake Bay and the fine line which indicates the course of the Susquehanna River. South I can see down the bay to where it joins the Atlantic at Hampton Roads. The Potomac isn't big any more. The country below looks like nothing but a crazy quilt of tan and green patches, with the fine line of the river like a tear in the cloth.

The bay and rivers are fine points of reference when you are so high above the earth. The sun is almost overhead, its rays silvering the water. To the westward a haze is beginning to obscure the mountains, but I can follow the course of the Potomac almost to Harper's Ferry.

The view is beautiful, fascinating, but I must get back to work. If I can get 5,000 feet more there will be no doubt of establishing a new record. But my optimism doesn't last long.

Several things happen simultaneously. In the first place the altimeter seems to stick at 38,000 feet. A cloud comes across my eyes.   I recognize the frost slowly beginning to form on the glass of my goggles.   No use trying to wipe it off.   I can't touch the inside of the glass where the frost is.   I hope it will clear up, but instead of clearing it grows steadily heavier.

Now I will have to rely upon the tiny holes bored in the glass. I am not entirely without use of my eyes, although my vision is restricted, so much so that it is impossible to see the horizon or to view the instruments closely.   I don't want to remove the goggles, but I have to.   I push them up on my forehead.

I am beginning to get pretty weak.   Humans don't belong in this altitude.   I need more oxygen and open the emergency valve, gulping down a good deep breath.

I feel somewhat better, but we are not climbing very fast. I have to put my head down in the cockpit behind the cowling. My eyes are freezing and very painful.   My right hand is beginning to get cold from holding the frigid stick, although the rest of my body is warm.

To return to the field now would be failure.   We will keep going as long as we can.   The altimeter must be frozen.   It seems to be sticking now at 39,000 feet.

I increase the angle of climb slightly.   This does not seem to help a great deal.   The time passes like hours before I push the altimeter up to 40,000 feet.   But I am not satisfied.   I try to climb higher.   My eyes are causing considerable trouble, so I push the goggles back down.   I don't want to injure them for a record.

I have to fly with my knees controlling the stick.   My left hand is busy holding the supercharger throttle.   Although the automatic spring, which would pull it closed and slow down the motor if I fell unconscious, is not heavy, it seems as if it were a heavy weight.

I hold my goggles with my right hand like a lady with her lorgnette. In this way I can break the wind and get an occasional glimpse about.

Still we do not climb. I am getting pretty impatient and weak. I feel a strange dizziness, anticipated but nevertheless annoying. I let the oxygen flow continually now through the emergency tube to be sure I do not faint for lack of it.

The plane already is wavering as if it cannot go higher. But I am determined to force it up at any cost. I stick the nose higher. This is not wise, I soon learn. Almost before I realize it the nose whips over and we are falling crazily in a spin. That was the plane's peak. We could go no higher.

Well, what of it, I think; let her spin; that lazy feeling is comfortable.

I let go the throttle of the supercharger. The motor slows down to idling speed. The air is so light and the controls so tightly frozen that we fall 2,000 feet before I work out of the spin. I spiral down in great circles, slowly, so there will be no ill effects to plane or pilot from the descent. My ears, though, ache from the growing pressure.

Now the field is coming into sight. The job is nearly done. I circle a few times and then slip down through the gully into the field. The men who have helped me come to greet me. I climb out again after an hour and twenty-four minutes in the air. It was worth it. I am feeling fine.

TWO TOUGH HOMBRES

An Intimate Historical Record of 246 Hours in the Air

L. MENDELL AND R. REINHART

TWO tough hombres (self-admitted) cramped in the small quarters of their Buhl biplane, the *Angeleno*, outrode fog and bumpy air in a small area west of Los Angeles to establish a duration refueling record which prior to the flight of the Army's *Question Mark* would have been thought impossible. Although this epochal flight has been eclipsed by the recent extended jaunt of the St. Louis *Robin*, it remains a noteworthy and spectacular performance—a real landmark in aerial progress.

Considerable newspaper space has been devoted to the fact that both plane and power slant were "second hand." They were, but it is worth noting that the engine which had already shown 450 hours, was completely rebuilt under supervision of W. E. Thomas, Western distributor for the Wright Corporation.

The gallant ship, with its crew, Loren Mendell and Roland Reinhart, came down to a perfect three point landing after sustained flight of 246 hours, 43 minutes and 32 seconds.

Here are presented some of the notes sent down by the flyers. They give the "feel" of the flight more competently than any mere description.

The first two were written by E. E. McManus, field manager of the Culver City Airport—the others fluttered from
the grimy hands of Pete and Loren.

Tuesday, July 2—afternoon contact.
Hello, Boys:—How are things going? Paul and I spent
the morning collecting things to fix up the "Pigeon" and
while we are in better shape than yesterday we have lots to
do. The papers have been calling up all morning and one of
the Associated Press wanted a 200-word story by Reinhart
for use on the coast. I told them I didn't know at this time
whether we could let them have it or not but write it anyway,
Pete, and we'll see what happens. You didn't date the note
you dropped this morning. Wish you would so that if they
are lost we will be able to keep them in order when they are
found. We are numbering them as they come in.

INSTRUCTION: When Slade lowers the contact line he will
next lower food or oil on the second length of rope. You can
bring it in with the first line. Unload it and then fasten on
to the rope whatever you want to return (food, cans, etc.) and
let Slade pull the bag back into the "Pigeon." BUT KEEP
YOUR LINE FASTENED so that he can use it to give you
the gas hose. After gassing you can drop the plumb or first
line on to the field so we can use it on next contact.

Follow Paul's instructions on morning contact. Best of
luck.   MAC.

Wednesday morning.
How do you like these nice clear mornings? Hope every-

thing is O.K. Let me know the first note you drop. The papers want everything they can get so write anything of interest that happens. New signals from the ground: Coming up to refuel you so stand by to get filled up. T on ground will point towards the place where the "Pigeon" was last seen. This is not the wind T but the one we are using in front of the hangars.

Had a man working all night on the "Pigeon" motor and he found plenty wrong but guess everything will be O.K. from now on. Will send up the papers and a note from Loren's girl when we contact for breakfast. Pacific Air Transport called up during the night telling us they were leaving their boundary, beacon, and landing lights on for you. Drop them a "thank you" note and we'll send it over to them. Thank Van Dusen for the dinner. Everybody is pulling for you and think you can make it. THE FIRST THREE DAYS ARE THE WORST. Give my best to any gulls or night owls you meet and keep going.

Best of luck.   MAC.

                                        July 2, 5:05 P.M.
Hey—Send up 150 gal. about 7:15 tonight—don't think we got very much of the last—Loren wants to know if the beacon will be on tonight. Will fly from the University City sign over our field to Lincoln Airways field. Have Slade nod his head if a light and shake it if not. P. S.—Was the Jap sore about the rope?

                                        LOREN AND PETE.

P. S.—Motor like a clock.

6:30 A.M.

Must have gas in the next 15 minutes. Contact above field, fog not very thick. Bring us two gal. water later on.

6:37 A.M.

Bring up 2 gal. water. We're dying of thirst.

7:30 A.M.

Mac—Send up some water in the monocoupe. We haven't had water since 12 last night. Thanks for the quick service. Our tanks weren't full last night. We thought they were. Oh, boy! She sure was hot up here last night.

(*Untimed*)

We are O.K.—a little tired. The fog raised havoc with us. The Pacific air turned on their beacon at 2. Send up 125 gal. gas in about 30 min. or so.

Motor running fine. Turning 1600 most of the time. I ordered a bottle of Syrup Pepsin yesterday, it wasn't sent up. Wish you'd see to it for me. Every time you let something down in a sack send a gallon of water. We ran out at 11 last night and like to have died before this morning. We'd rather have water than food. The coupe is the hot stuff for contact. (*Food was delivered frequently from a Monocoupe.*)

June 3, 9:30 A.M.

Thanks for the quick service this morning. It was a close call. We didn't have as much gas last night as we thought we had and I never saw such a thick fog in all my life as it was this morning. Say, canny Scot, we don't want any more second hand batteries; no light at all last night, only for 30 minutes. Wish you'd have a white band to place in front of the "Pigeon" about 5 minutes before it takes off so I will know and not miss it. I almost missed it last night. Please watch that. We want a full load of gas tonight, no more chances like that for me.

June 3, 3 P.M.

Van Dusen Drug Co.—Thanks a lot for your splendid service; everything is good; sure do like the orange juice. Send more.

(*Same time*)

Pacific Air Transport—Thanks a lot for the beacon. Would appreciate it if you could leave it on each night; it is a great help.

(*Five minutes later*)

Mac—Your note about the gas; I will have to have more than that; what I now have will only run me until about 5 P.M. and I'd like to have full tanks to start the night with. If you could bring up 125 gal. each time that would be O.K. but bring whatever you can; if we have to make three contacts we can; however, I think you could bring 100 one time and 125 another and that would be enough. Don't forget to send up the batteries for lights and some orange juice, but no solid foods; drinks seem better. I have been sick all day but feel better now. The coupe is O.K. for sacks; don't send any oil until morning; we have enough. Send some "Lucky Strikes" for Pete.

5 P.M.

Tell Paul to throttle down a little more on contact. Both main tanks and wing tanks are full now; no more oil until tomorrow A.M.; motor like a clock, plugs O.K. Wish this fog and rough air would let up. Loren and I both sick.

6:30 P.M.

Bring up 50 at 7 P.M. Stay east out of fog. Bring batteries for navigation lights—get regular hot shots. Those last night burned nearly an hour; after that we were dark. Thanks for fags and thank Ruth and Jane for the cake.

July 4, 7:25 A.M.

Bring up 100 gal. gas 1 hour from time; contact between field and Mt. Wilson. Fog about 800 feet thick. Contact you above fog. Engine O.K.; both tired but feeling better. One hundred feet ceiling now; if it raises to 1500 we will contact under fog.

(*By this time the fliers apparently had lost all idea of time, for the next and longest message was dated June 4. It was dropped at 2 p.m. on July 4.*)

Hello, Gang:—Well, all is O.K. Today is the first that Pete and myself have felt like anything. We feel good now and eat some for the first time since being up. We have felt bad but seems as the old Whirlwind kind of likes it. It's been purring to us just like an old Tom cat ever since we have been up and I hope it continues to do so for 400 hrs., and it sure likes the taste of gas and oil. The old Buhl is O.K., only it's lazy; don't like to get up so high; does pretty well to 2,000 ft., then gets cranky. Tell the boys I am sorry about the sack this morning but the reason I couldn't make contact was because it was hanging down and I was afraid of getting it in the prop or tail group. Always let me get in position before letting it down. The coupe is O.K. for transfer if they will remember this. Tell Paul his speed is fine, just right. That seems to be the most important thing in airplane hosing.

Order same weather without fog. Had to fly 3 hrs. blind last night and it is not too good a feeling to have to plane down through it in the mornings. Too many mountains. We want to thank all for their kindness and for your extreme confidence in us two poor old reprobates. It's great to have such friends and we'll not forget. Send up 1 hr. after this is dropped, 125 gal. gas and then at 7 P.M. 125 more. We carry enough for 14 hours when full. Don't think our capacity is as much as we figured. We are using around 16 gal. per hour. Send up 2 gal. oil, 2 gal. water; we have 3 gal. oil left. Send up map of California and some more newspapers; guess that is all. Thanks.

July 4, 3:30 P.M.

Everything fine here except fog at night; poor stuff to fly in if you ask me. Both feeling much better. Let Loren ask for food and gas; otherwise it doesn't give us an opportunity for rest in the evening and makes us sleepy and tired for the night. Both of us dozed off last night. Hope you have the Buhl insured. Love and kisses.

July 4, 5:30 P.M.

Bring up 50 at 7:15 . . . with all tanks full we have enough for 14 hrs.; must contact by 9:30 A.M. at latest. Will contact for 10 minutes for radio; is there any money in it? Our radio won't work. Lights shorted somewhere, need battery tomorrow. Paul, fly a little lower on this contact, due to heavy load.

July 5, 7 A.M.

Good morning, everybody. We are fine, all O.K. Had a nice night, rested well and old Whirlwind did her stuff . . . also advise if Cleveland fliers are still up and if so how long.

8:30 A.M.

Good morning, gang. God bless you! Send up some rags, too; not too many. All's well, both feeling fine—had a good night. Think the worst part over physically. Motor good. Plugs O.K. Lubricating system O.K. Loren says wait till 9:30 to make contact, thinks it will be clear by then.

Beginning to have hopes of success now.

Had bum air for a while, couldn't get over 1,000 ft.

1 P.M.

Well, all is well so far. We both feel good and can eat some. I think that was the first time in my life I ever lost my appetite. Looks like the Cleveland fliers will get there first. Well, hope

they don't set it too high.   As to gas, there is only one way
to do it right and that is to bring it up as we order it, otherwise we are flying around with a lot of extra weight.
We have to fly almost wide open at night but this can't be
helped of course.   That gets my goat about the D of C.   We
have never flown over town at all except when it was foggy
the other morning, and I couldn't have helped that if they
was to cut my head off.   Wish you'd explain to them that I
am not trying to break any regulations at all, and it was only
in case of emergency that I flew over town at all.   Send up
another can of rocker arm grease today.

5:30 P.M.

Paul, you'll have to fly just a little slower.   You pull away
from us all the time.   Loren says if you do settle a bit, it won't
hurt.   We were wide open and you were still too fast.   Coffee,
orange juice, sandwiches.

9:40 P.M.

Just heard over radio that Cleveland fliers have broken
record.   Wire them our congratulations.

July 6, 6:50 A.M.

If we get 110 gal. each time we'll only have to make three
contacts a day . . . as to food, only send us a little coffee
and about 8 sandwiches a day . . . we have so little room
here that with so much stuff we have little room to sleep or
even to stretch out.

July 6, 1 P.M.

At the time of the flight of the "Question Mark" the uppermost question in the minds of the people was whether it was an endurance of the plane or the men. . . . After passing the 100-hour mark in the air it is our belief that it is not a test of men's endurance, providing they have made ample preparations for comfortable rest. Outside of our digestive system we have felt normal. In fact after having become used to the grind we feel better than before the start because then we were working almost night and day preparing for the flight. The test of the motor is to the extremes they must run constantly and without alteration to adjustments, as a motor flying three or four hours at a time would have. My first impressions were that time would drag very slowly but we find time seems to fly. We sleep a while on a comfortable bed we have and fly a while. We do not like the foggy weather. The first two nights were awful. We had to get above the fog and fly blind, or in other words without any landmarks. It was on one of these mornings that I came through the fog where I thought I would be over the ocean, but instead I came out in the center of Hollywood some 200 feet above the town and had to fall back into the fog to keep from hitting the mountain. I was low on gas and knew that I must reach the field and order gas or crack up, so I flew low over town staying under the fog. . . . We were lucky and reached the field and dropped a note telling of our plight. Pilot Durfee came up in a small ship through the fog and delivered us five gallons in a can, enough to last until the refueling ship came up.

As to time, we found that circling a spot is better than taking trips to places because in going to San Diego or elsewhere one keeps his mind on getting there and as a result watching your watch. In keeping close to the field one forgets all this. We hope to stay up until our motor stops and we hope this happens in the day time after we have put several hours on to the present record.

Date: "Aw, I forget."
4:25 P.M.

Bring ½ gal. coal oil and squirt can in the morning. Both of us feel fine, got used to it now—we will stay as long as the engine does; might drop a grapefruit in the morning and a sandwich or two.

OK—MNX.

Sunday, July 7, 7:45 A.M.

. . . We have only 1½ hrs. gas left; don't be too long. Do not send any oil—all O.K. If you can stretch that gas to 110 gallons, three contacts is all we will have to make a day.

2 P.M.

With a full load we have got to run it most wide open for 3 or 4 hrs., so stand by early in the morning for refueling. Do not bring any more than I have ordered . . . and how about that coal oil we ordered yesterday. A valve stuck for a while and we didn't have anything to loosen it up with. (Paul, you are a real "Pigeon" flyer—keep it up!) I will write those letters as soon as I can find time. We don't have as much extra time as you'd think for.

NOTE—*No notes of consequence were dropped on the eighth. The fliers made routine requests for fuel.*

July 9, 2 P.M.

. . . I think it would be a good idea to have a signal system (for refueling) like Pete and I do. I tie a rope around my leg. He takes the other end and when he gives me one pull that means to go ahead a little faster; two jerks to back up; three when he contacts, and a quick succession to pull away. You'd be surprised at how it works. The day we got the hose too close to the prop I forgot to tie the rope on my leg and that was what happened. So if you had a rope down to Slade he could signal you to slow down. It won't hurt if you do settle some. I'll keep out of your way . . . if you could have Slade let you know you could throttle some, and as your load is partly gone you would not settle.

3:30 P.M.

Send us a quart of rubbing alcohol. Send me up a $1.50 watch. Mine went haywire. Set it right time. Motor running like a clock now.

July 10, 5:15 A.M.

At 6:45 deliver me some gas and 5 gal. oil.

3 P.M.

To the Baldwin Locomotive Works
    and Mack Truck Co.

Dear Madam:

I am writing you this letter in appreciation of the great service rendered us by one of your 1742 model "Pigeons." If it had six more Libertys it could get off with 50 gallons of gasoline. I am not boasting for what it does but for what it tries to do. It snorts, groans and puffs and that's all the Texas steer could do.

Its take-off is remarkable. That is, it is remarkable if it takes off. Pigeon Pilot Paul Whittier in one tried to take off in a short field five miles long and almost got over a three-wire fence.

And I can safely say in closing that I am sure there would be more of them in use if they could get high enough to pass the Department of Commerce rules for low flying.

I wish to state that the rust-proof steel plating has only rusted halfway through in all these years of service. Hoping you can build better barns in the future, I am,

                            Disgustedly yours,

5 P.M.

Say listen—Once and for all, confound it, it took us a week to get up to this point and if you think we're coming down today, you're crazy. And that's not all—we're two tough hombres. Don't worry about us before you have to.

THE "YARDSTICKER" SAILPLANE

How to Build and Fly One

BY R. E. DOWD

IN the August issue of AERO DIGEST we took up the description of the Windjammer paper glider and by this time you have doubtless some splendid flights on record. We presume a good many hundreds of pounds of paper in the form of Windjammers have been cruising the air during the last month. More power to you, Boy! Let's hear all about your records, but in the meantime here's a nifty sailplane for your next model.

It doesn't seem possible that any boy has escaped hearing the time-worn pun, "Did you ever see a horse fly?" or that other one, "Ever see a board walk?" We knew you had, but here's a new one: "Did you ever see a yardstick fly?" We have, and we're going to tell you all about how to make the neatest sailplane patterned after the famous German record-breaking soarers, all from an everyday yellow yardstick, the kind your hardware dealer gives away to advertise stoves and other merchandise. The name sailplane has become used as a result of the wonderful glider performances of German experimenters with gliders "sailing" on rising currents of air.

Oh! that reminds us of what the "wise cracker" said: "I have a yardstick but I don't use it as a *rule*." As a matter of fact we're not either. We're going to use it for wings and fuselage, so let's go! Here is what you need:

MATERIALS FOR YOUR SAILPLANE

Only 6 items:

One soft wood, everyday, county fair yardstick. (These usually are stained yellow and carry advertisements.)

One piece of tough cardboard, about the thickness of ordinary name cards or correspondence cards.

One piece of stiff wire (music wire is best), about .020 inch in diameter.

One or two small rubber bands.

Some glue or cement and some thin shellac.

A strip of sheet metal about $\frac{1}{2}$ inch wide, $\frac{1}{32}$ inch thick and approximately 2 inches long. (Steel, tin, lead, brass or anything handy will do.)

Tools you should have are:

A plane (small block plane preferred), a sharp knife or razor blade, a pair of scissors, a pair of pliers, a small brush for shellacking, some fine sandpaper, and a few pieces of broken window glass for scraping.

Well, there's nothing very hard about getting the material and tools together, so let's get started on the building. One more thing before we start. Let's resolve to do some real fine workmanship in every model we build. Good workmanship pays high rewards when you take your finished model out to fly. It is wonderful what fine work can be turned out by willing hands if only the decision is made at the beginning to do a careful job. Sorry to lecture, boys, but you'll be twice as proud of the finished model and she'll fly like a demon if you'll just do a nice job of it.

The standard yardstick measures ⅜₁₆ inch thick and 1⅛ inches wide. Guess we don't have to say how long it is, do we? Well, first plane one side flat, just lightly so that the coloring is removed. This will allow you to inspect the grain and to select the best 18 inches of length in the piece. Now cut this section out for your main plane. Notice we do not call it a wing, because strictly speaking a wing is only one-half of a plane. In other words, we have a plane made up of right

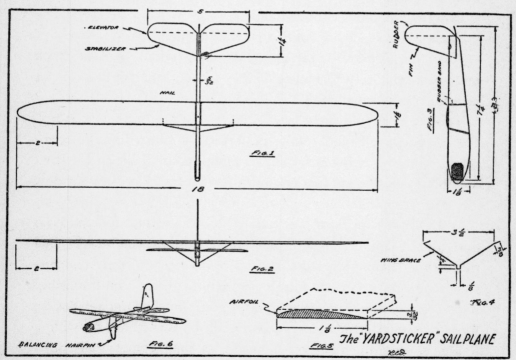

The "YARDSTICKER" SAILPLANE

and left wings. Airplanes are so often called 'planes for short that there is a tendency to call the actual plane a wing.

Now having one surface flat, we plane the piece down to a $\frac{3}{32}$-inch thickness. That's pretty thin but you can do it by holding one end fast to a flat board and planing away from you. If you do this, reversing the ends frequently, you'll soon have the old yardstick looking like a brand new piece of wood.

Now for the airfoil section. Does that sound too complicated? See figure 5, which is a view of the stick and how it should be planed down. The shape is called an airfoil, since it is designed to obtain certain reactions from the air. The bottom is flat, the front or leading edge is thick, while the rear or trailing edge is thin. In full-size airplanes each wing section or airfoil has a special name or number and designers choose them very carefully to get the best results. Colonel Lindbergh's *Spirit of St. Louis* had a wing curve or section known as Clark Y. This is quite similar to ours but somewhat thicker to give room for spars.

Well, just shape your curve and when it is all uniform from tip to tip, plane the tips up on the bottom as shown in the front view (figure 2). The thickness at the very tip should be only $\frac{1}{32}$ inch. Next make a paper pattern of the elliptical end shape and cut the tips to correct form. Wing tips can be of many different shapes without a very great change in efficiency but the one shown is not only efficient, but will not split easily in bad landings.

The plane is all finished now except for the rubber band

notches and the two small holes for the wire brace to the fuselage. The holes can be made with an ordinary common pin gripped in a pair of pliers and forced into the leading edge carefully. They should be about ⅜ inch deep.

Before we leave the building of the plane we should learn about aspect ratio, which simply means the length or span of a plane, divided by the width or chord. Six is considered more or less standard (18-inch span, 3-inch chord) for aspect ratios, but sailplanes use them much higher to get greater efficiencies. Our little plane has an aspect ratio of about 16, which is quite high.

Next Build the Fuselage

Just plane, scrape or sandpaper the coloring from a piece of the yardstick 7¼ inches long and then cut to the shape shown. The corners, except directly under the plane, should be nicely rounded off to reduce air resistance. With a thin-bladed knife or a safety razor blade cut the slots for the stabilizer and fin at the rear of the fuselage. Don't try to make the slot in one cut. Be patient and cut again and again lightly but deeper each time.

If you care to, you can exercise a whole lot of individuality in making new forms of fins and stabilizers. All designers do this and if you have any special shape you like you can design to suit yourself. However, the area must be kept very closely to what is shown on the drawing and perhaps you better stick to the form shown for your first model. The fin is just half of the stabilizer and both parts are cemented in place using glue or Ambroid cement.

Let's see, what else do we need? Oh, yes, the wing brace. Just bend the wire into the form shown at the bottom of the fuselage and then bend so as to fit the holes in the leading edge of the wing. Better be very careful in bending for it must be quite accurate and true.

Now we can attach the plane to the fuselage using a single flat head nail about ½ inch long. The nail used in the lid of a cigar box is just the right size. Everything is now assembled except the ballast and we cannot determine that until the whole model has been shellacked or completely finished with some thin waterproofing lacquer, because the finish will change the balance.

BALANCE YOUR SAILPLANE BEFORE FLYING

The center of gravity or the center of "balance" must come ⅜ inch from the leading edge. Open out a hairpin and file the ends to a knife edge and apply enough weight to the nose of the fuselage to balance the plane exactly at that point. (See figure 6.) Cut the metal strip to the correct size. Pinch temporarily to the nose of the fuselage and the final attachment can be made by turning the corners down so that they clinch into the wood.

A small piece of rubber or a rubber head tack may be used as part of the weight and will be found a great protection when your "Yardsticker" sails into a window or bumps Billy Jones on the nose.

Now for the fun! Your "Yardsticker" is ready to make the first flight. You'd better make the first trials in pretty calm weather so that the disturbing gusts of air won't bother making the final adjustments. If there should be a slight breeze be sure to launch directly against the wind. When we made the Windjammer we learned how to adjust for fore and aft balance. The rule is simple. If the model noses up, reduce the amount of upturn on the elevators. If it noses down, increase the amount of upturn. If she turns to the right or left quickly after launching, be sure you are not "banking" it as you launch it forward. If it turns and you are launching correctly, check up on your rudder. It should be absolutely true. If banking still persists, try warping the whole plane, by twisting it. Of course the trailing edge should be warped *down* on the wing which is on the *inside* of the turn. When she's all set, give her a good hard launch with a full swing of the arm. Up she'll go—not 20 or 30 feet—but 75 to 100—and fast! You'll get the surprise of your life if you've been making light "floater" models. Now, for some stunts:

Loop—Launch level directly into the wind, pointing the nose upward.

Right Turn—Launch into the wind with right bank. (Right wing down.)

Left Turn—Same, but bank to the left.

Figure Eight—Adjust rudder by bending to the left (looking at the model from the tail) and launch with a right bank.

Soaring—Find a rising current, such as a gentle breeze blowing up a hill, and launch easily into the wind. Study the adjustment carefully to keep the flight straight. Turning loses height and you want to conserve all the height you can. Soaring is an art requiring active control for extended flights, but your little "Yardsticker" will give you a treat in short duration soaring if you'll take care in the adjusting. Let's hear all about your flights.

Here are the high spots to remember: 1—Sailplane. 2—Airfoil. 3—Aspect Ratio. 4—Fuselage. 5—Stabilizer. 6—Elevator. 7—Fin. 8—Rudder. 9—Banking. 10—Soaring.

SOME RECENT SPECTACULAR FLIGHTS

BY ROBERT B. RENFRO

PUBLIC interest in flying has been keener this year than at any time previous, except when Colonel Lindbergh made his immortal flight to Paris in May, 1927. A rapid succession of spectacular flights in 1929 has done much to alter the layman's thoughts so that he is no longer simply half-curious; he now has a desire to participate. Although he may not yet be ready to adopt the airplane as his principal means of transportation, he is anxious to experience the sensation of flying in short hops from his local airport. And, once he goes up, he becomes (whether he realizes it or not) a very probable patron of the airlines a short time hence.

Although this attitude arises somewhat from a growing knowledge of the real safety of the modern airplane, attested by millions of miles of reliable airline operation, it is partially the outcome of successful flights which are more or less dramatic in character. In fact, it is the most obvious result of such flights, but by no means the most important outcome thereof.

Quite often, however, as much value derives from unsuccessful flights as from those which attain their original objectives. In the several transatlantic attempts this season, this point has been amply demonstrated. The creditable flights of the *Pathfinder* and the *Yellow Bird* across the Atlantic

Ocean were less significant in some respects than the frustrated effort of Major Franco and his companions in the Dornier-Wal, *Numancia*, which is discussed later in this article. We omit details of the flight of the French Bernard monoplane, *Yellow Bird*, since they were fully covered in the July issue of AERO DIGEST and since they closely parallel those of the Bellanca, *Pathfinder*.

On July 8th at 8:49 A.M., Eastern Daylight Time, with Roger Q. Williams as pilot and Lewis A. Yancey as navigator, the *Pathfinder* took off from Old Orchard, Maine, to fly to Rome, Italy, an estimated distance of 4,700 miles. Because of the prospect of favorable tail winds, the fuel load was reduced at the last minute from 500 to 450 gallons, which of course made the take-off easier. After flying continuously for approximately thirty-one and a half hours and covering 3,400 miles, the Bellanca monoplane landed at Albericia Aerodrome, four miles from Santander, Spain. Shortage of gasoline brought the ship down before it reached its proposed destination. It landed only a short distance beyond where the *Yellow Bird* was forced to descend for the same reason.

Next day the monoplane flew to Rome, where Williams and Yancey were received with a tremendous ovation.

Disregarding the mishaps and delays of the *Green Flash*, in which Williams and Yancey originally intended to fly the Atlantic, let us consider what these facts indicate. More than anything else, both the *Pathfinder* and the *Yellow Bird* emphasized again that, given fairly favorable weather conditions, the modern airplane is fully capable of spanning the

Atlantic non-stop. The former plane demonstrated once more the well-known quality of the Bellanca design and the Wright Whirlwind engine. (Whirlwind engines have been used in six of the seven successful eastward crossings by American planes, and Bellancas have crossed twice.) The presence of the American fliers in Rome has probably served to strengthen Italian friendliness toward us. Indeed, therein lies one of the greatest benefits of the flight. Knowledge of weather conditions over the Atlantic will probably be augmented, since Yancey is a skilled meteorologist and navigator, and ought now to be able to make some further important contributions to those sciences.

Although the *Pathfinder* was equipped with no radio, the fact that the French plane carried one suggests some interesting thoughts. Because ships at sea did not know when to expect radio signals from the plane, too few established communication with the *Yellow Bird* to determine its location with useful accuracy at any time during the flight. If the plane had suddenly been forced to descend, the duration of its S O S would probably have been too brief for a ship's radio operator to locate the plane with his direction finder. It seems plausible, therefore, that a system should be devised by which ships at sea could expect radio messages from a transatlantic plane at regular intervals and at a designated frequency and thus know its approximate location at all times. Then, in case of an emergency, it could be found more easily.

Since the question inevitably arises in this connection, it

is appropriate to ask, did either the *Yellow Bird* or the *Pathfinder* increase the possibility that we shall soon have regular transatlantic flight schedules for mail, express and paying passengers? Yes, somewhat; all such flights do.

Yet experiences of Major Ramon Franco are perhaps a more important contribution toward that end. The fact that the Dornier-Wal remained afloat on the open ocean for a week before rescue came is an incontestable argument for the flying boat. Despite consistently rough seas, which on June 27th raged all day with particular fury, the hull of the Dornier proved absolutely seaworthy. When one considers this severe test of the seaplane, the use of land planes for trans-oceanic flying appears extremely hazardous, even foolhardy. When airplanes are put into regular service across such great bodies of water as the Atlantic, they undoubtedly will be huge flying boats, more navigable on the sea's surface, with far stouter hulls than the present ones, and with from twelve to twenty engines. The first plane to approach this type is the new 100-passenger Dornier Do. X., powered with twelve Hornet engines, which was test-flown in Germany in July.

In mentioning pioneering flights between Europe and America, we cannot disregard the two attempts this year to accomplish the passage by the northern route,—Canada, Greenland, Iceland and Scandinavia. Both Parker Cramer in the *"Untin" Bowler* and Ahrenberg in a Junkers met with unforeseen difficulties. But their misfortunes do not disprove the feasibility of the northern route, and it may be that, with an enlarged knowledge of conditions in that region, regular flying can be established across it.

Transatlantic fliers this year, however, are greatly outnumbered by those hoping to break the refueling endurance record. Indeed, refueling flights have become a current fad, undertaken by commercial pilots in every part of the nation and backed by nothing much more than their determination and the enthusiasm of the local populace. And therein rests both the strength and the weakness of these attempts. Undertaken individually, these endurance flights have utilized standard commercial equipment, usually slightly revamped for the immediate purpose, and have put it through the crucial test of protracted service. Many of the planes and engines already had had many hours in the air before they began their long endurance grinds; rarely were new or specially built planes used. Those which stood up under the strain attested adequately to the high character of their construction; those which failed defined more clearly what weaknesses need correction. If the causes of the breakdown of engines and planes in these long flights can be studied first hand by competent persons, we may rightfully expect the elimination of many faults and therefore a general progression in design.

Since May, the record has changed hands three times. Still one of the queries which the Army *Question Mark* sought to answer in January remains an uncertainty. What is the ultimate endurance of the modern airplane? Since Robbins and Kelly in the *Fort Worth* finally landed because of acci-

dental damage to the propeller and not because of human
exhaustion or inherent weakness of plane or engine, their
experience added some enlightenment but did not give a final
answer. When Roy Mitchell and Byron Newcomb brought
their Stinson, *City of Cleveland*, to earth after 174 hours and
59 seconds in the air, their plane and engine were still in good
condition. Loren Mendell and R. B. Reinhart remained aloft
in their Buhl Airsedan, *Angeleno*, for 246 hours, 43 minutes,
2 seconds, and finally landed because of tail flutter resulting
from accidental damage. The question of the absolute endurance of flying equipment will have to be answered by future
flights.

Although refueling flights conducted locally are of great
value, we can expect much greater benefits when they are carried out on a national scope. Wherever these attempts have
been made recently, two men have flown day after day over the
same place,—Robbins and Kelly over Fort Worth, Mitchell
and Newcomb in the vicinity of Cleveland, and Reinhart
and Mendell near Los Angeles. The present record-holders,
in the Wright-powered Buhl, covered an estimated distance
of 19,760 miles at an average speed of 80 miles per hour. But
all these figures will mean much more when they can be converted into airline distance. The Army Air Corps is the only
group which thus far has made practical application of refueling; e.g., refueling of bombardment planes on long-distance
missions during the recent Air Corps maneuvers. To demonstrate its commercial practicability is the next logical step.
Refueling ought to be utilized for flying from coast to coast

Army and Navy Observation and Pursuit Planes in
Formation Maneuvers such as seen in Cleveland,
Ohio, during the 1929 National Air Races

across the continent, where all the conditions of practical flights would be encountered. Such experimental flights, plus an increased average speed, would comprise a decided progression toward a desirable transcontinental non-stop transport service.

Individual, local enterprise would, of course, be inadequate to accomplish this. It would require more complete organization and stronger financing, which only an airline operator, a large manufacturer or the Government could furnish. But it would fully justify the effort and expense involved in an undertaking of this character.

Non-stop transcontinental flights by refueling are more adaptable to commercial purposes than non-refueling flights because they permit of greater pay loads. Their potentialities do not in any way detract, however, from the tremendous significance of Captain Frank Hawk's one-stop flight from New York to Los Angeles and return. Although Captain Hawks used a standard commercial ship, the Wasp-powered Lockheed Air Express, his flight is perhaps more important to military than to commercial aeronautics. His performance has given us the idea of the potential mobility of our air force. Assuming that both our coasts were under attack at the same time and that a heavy offensive was suddenly launched in one sector, an air force which could be assembled quickly by sending large squadrons non-stop from all sections of the country would be of inestimable value. Captain Hawks and others have shown what possibilities exist in that respect. The Army Air Corps, recognizing the military value of such a flight, had already assigned Captain Ross G. Hoyt to undertake a similar round-trip coast to coast flight.

When Captain Hawks made the remarkable time of 19 hours, 10 minutes, 32 seconds, for the East-to-West trip and 17 hours, 38 minutes, 16 seconds, for the return flight (a total flying time of 36 hours, 48 minutes, 48 seconds), the Army cancelled its projected flight because its contention that the trip could be made in 36 hours was sufficiently proved.

As we go to press, the refueling endurance record has been broken once more. The ship, in this instance, is a Curtiss-Robin powered with a Challenger engine which turns up 170 horsepower at 1,800 revolutions per minute. The *St. Louis-Robin*, as the plane is called, is being piloted by Dale (Red) Jackson and Forest O'Brine and, at this time, has been in the air more than three hundred and twenty hours. The pilots contend that they will continue to fly until they reach the 500-hour mark.

Jackson and O'Brine, who took off from Lambert-St. Louis Field at 9:17 A.M. on July 13, established a new record when on July 23 at 5:00:2 P.M. they had been flying 247 hours, 43 minutes, 2 seconds, or an hour longer than Mendell and Reinhart had remained aloft. Immediately thousands of the air-minded citizens of St. Louis burst into an uproar of enthusiasm and celebration. Large crowds thronged Lambert Field and, escorted by two squadrons of planes, the *St. Louis-Robin* circled the downtown section while factory whistles sounded their congratulations.

This flight differs from other recent endurance attempts in that it is not an individual enterprise, but is sponsored by the Curtiss-Robertson Airplane Manufacturing Company, which produces the Curtiss-Robin monoplane. What factors will eventually cause this plane to land are still a matter of conjecture as this is being written, and, therefore, the full significance of the company's direct connection with this flight remains uncertain. Although reports are yet incomplete, it appears certain, however, that such backing has had some effect in this flight, for it undoubtedly has provided a more thoroughly organized ground crew and it afforded highly efficient facilities for servicing the ship before the flight. But whether or not this circumstance has had a far-reaching influence, the quality of the engine is undoubtedly the most essential element.

This flight becomes even more impressive when one considers that before the *Question Mark* made its flight last January the American refueling record was 37½ hours, made by Captain Lowell Smith of the Army in 1923. Unless something unforeseen occurs, the *St. Louis-Robin* bids fair to demonstrate, not only the high efficiency of the Challenger engine, but also the ultimate endurance of the medium powered aircraft engine in its present stage of development.

AMERICA FROM A SKIMMING PLANE

BY T. J. C. MARTYN

Based on the author's recent flight across the continent, the following article gives descriptive impressions of the immense and varied domain of the United States as seen and felt by the air passenger.

THE spanning of the United States as a bird on the wing might span it marks a milestone in the affairs of men. It is not merely that the airplane has made distance as fleet as the hour, not only that it has brought the Pacific some three days nearer to the Atlantic; its greater significance is to be vaguely sensed in the changes which regular air travel will doubtless compel. One of those changes will be in getting used to seeing the earth from a strange angle, viewing it, so to speak, through a bird's eye. In this age of speed we have been accustomed to seeing a landscape roar past the window of a train. In the new era of speed which the airplane is opening we shall become accustomed to seeing at one coup d'oeil a hundred square miles of terrain and seeing it for longer than is possible from any other known means of locomotion, despite a speed twice as fast as an express train.

A wide view of the earth, a sense of its size, is responsible for this paradox; for, from a train, you gaze horizontally and see only a narrow strip of countryside and see it at the most for a minute or so; from a plane you gaze straight downward or upward almost to the horizontal, and, since a plane is narrower than a train, you can allow your eyes to sweep the horizon in two almost complete semicircles. You look downward and see the ground moving swiftly backward; you look out and see a waterfall in the distance for five or ten minutes; and, flying at 2,000 or 3,000 feet, never for a moment are you conscious of traveling at a terrific speed, because the altitude robs the mind and cheats the eye.

It is trite to speak of the United States as enormous, of its more than 3,000,000 square miles of land and water. Every traveler knows that it takes between four and five days to cross its girth from coast to coast, some 3,000 miles. But none of these things means much to us. We speak glibly of 3,000,000 square miles, as we indeed speak glibly of 30,000,000 light years, without having the remotest conception of what the figures encompass. When you can fly at 100 miles an hour and cover with ease more than 1,000 miles of country between dawn and dusk, and always before you there stretches an endless and varied topography, then indeed is the magnitude of this country seen and sensed in something like its true perspective.

Seen from above, the United States in not only a huge but a powerfully impressive country. It expresses a hundred moods and rarely expresses them twice in the same way. As it is seen changingly from an airplane, it is not always a beautiful country, but it has its moments of sublimity; it is by no means an ugly country, but there are spots that are hideous. And it has its drab reaches over which the view is endlessly the same. But everywhere it is impressive; even from the air it looks the land of golden opportunity it is.

A transcontinental flight is something of a lesson in comparative geography and an experience rich in its rewards. Hour after hour new sights come rolling up from beyond the ever-receding horizon and in various sectors of the country those sights are as different as the sky is from the earth. There is the industrial East, an area spotted by the toil of man; the agricultural Middle West, a panorama of richly colored fields; the great plains, arid, burned and sparsely populated; the mountains of the West, vistas of majesty and splendor.

I—THE INDUSTRIAL EAST

Soaring up from Newark on a fine day you pass over an area that looks as if some fabulous god had snorted fire and burned the ground below black and brown. Press your face close to the window of your plane and look straight down, and there, 2,000 feet below, is a railroad desert inhabited by steaming locomotives pulling mile-long trains, for all the world like the heads of caterpillars laboriously drawing their long bodies behind them. It is a dreary region of brown and black, criss-crossed with shiny steel rails and pocked by clouds of steam and smoke.

Look to the east and you see the busy waterfront of New Jersey. A group of factories lift up their belching smokestacks to the sky against a background of pale silver water

faintly mirroring the sun. An incongruous, grimy scene where
ugly freighters cleave the upper bay in search of wharves stacked
untidily with giant cranes and the burdens they dutifully
carry from ship to shore. Look northward ever so slightly
and another great wilderness of railroad yards stretches out
to Jersey City, a begrimed and lusty child of industrialism. In
the early morning a score of electric trains are scurrying toward
New York. Here and there a blackened bridge spans a railroad track or some turbid stream. A tunnel opens wide its
mouth and swallows train after train or seemingly spits them
out into the open, a veritable ogre of modern times. An impressive picture, nevertheless, of the industrial East at its worst,
the more impressive because not a sound reaches you as you
gaze downward and sideways at this sprawling desolation of
nature. Overhead is the benign blue sky; beneath a pall that
flings defiance to the sun.

Past a swamp enlivened by the flashing colors of brightly
hued posters which line the railroad tracks, the green country
beckons and the shimmering Hudson spreads far into the north.
Your plane has now caught up with the view, so to speak;
for the chiaroscuro of the industrial regions you were gazing
at a few minutes before lies below. Beyond, across the Hudson,
rises pinnacled Manhattan. It would require a poet with
the imagination of a Shelley, the pen of a Tennyson and the
ink of a Shakespeare to do justice to the sight which greets
you. The groundling's paeans of praise sung in honor of the
city's skyline, if they told to the full its beauty and its virtues
as he can see them, would be prosaic in comparison with the

lyrics that a view from the air of the metropolis seems to merit.
Your route is up the Hudson and so you leave Manhattan a
mile or so to the right. If you allowed your imagination to
slip, you might see the city as a colossal Venice, for its piers,
sticking out into the Hudson like so many match sticks, give
the impression of a city built upon piles, with the piers as the
supporting cross members. But it is just a fleeting thought.

At the Battery end of the island, cathedrals of masonry
rise which outrival nature's cathedral rocks rising grandly
in the wilderness in far-off New Mexico. You look at this
massed mountain of buildings at an angle of about forty-five
degrees and view it from the top instead of the bottom, and
yet you miss nothing of the skyline effect, for the serried heights
of the tall monuments to business dwarf their background and
stand out aloof and majestic. Toward midtown the mountains become hills, with here and there a towering pinnacle,
but right in the center of the island the buildings dart upward
into mighty peaks. Sun-caught, they appear in chrome and
white and brown, silhouetted against the sky. Never is the
grandeur of the skyscraper seen more grandly, never does
it seem more to justify its name than when seen from the air.

One cannot speak of the industrial East as an immense
barren region devoted to drab industrialism and conquered
in its name. It is too big a region to be labeled. Between
the hives of industry lie green fields, huge blue and green lakes,
tree-clad mountains and winding rivers. But every now and
then, at Albany, at Pittsburgh, at Buffalo, to name a few great
centers, a fuming patch of industry spreads out like a boiling

blot of ink on the landscape.   Here it may be a forest of smoke-stacks pouring out an all-enveloping black cloud; there a row of sombre warehouses facing a front yard of railroad lines; or here again a silvered gas tank may mirror the spirit of the region.   Everywhere around, rows of uniform drab little houses; everywhere smoke, sometimes dense and sometimes hazy; everywhere stark efficiency manifested in living power noiselessly at work.

But it is not all like that.   There are other towns and vil-lages, sleepy and undefiled, gently touched with color, here a little red, there a splash of white, with an awning of dark patches marking perhaps a thousand roofs; and every now and then, sometimes in the most unexpected places, the plane roars over a country estate.   A great house, perhaps, standing serenely in the midst of immaculate gardens, with even the trees forming a patterned relief.   A tennis court seen from far on high, its surface green, white or even red, with little figures in white, for all the world like dolls, racing to and fro. Straight down below, perhaps half a mile, a swimming pool, its green or blue tiles reflecting a translucent glory through the water.   In a flash, it seems, it has gone, and a minute or two later your plane is brushing over a mountain top and you catch a vista of country sweeping out into the distance—a landscape that has defied the march of time and the hand of man.

Where New York is compact, making up for its restricted area in the height of its buildings, other towns and cities sprawl over large areas.   Not that the skyscraper ever disappears;

the humblest town or city would indeed consider itself poor
without one tall building. Manhattan rises into pinnacles
in proud isolation, but around it on every side there stretches
an amazing conglomeration of low buildings, broken in Jersey
City and in Brooklyn by a few frowning turrets. Smaller
cities cluster their buildings into a business sector and then
spread their industries, their fine residences and their humbler
homes in all directions. The result is that they appear larger
than they really are. Manhattan is .remarkably free from the
smirch of industry; she leaves the manufacturing mostly
to her backyard neighbors and gives evidence of being mainly
interested in business. In the other towns of the East industry
is always plainly evident on the outskirts, and long before you
see the city proper you are aware of its existence by the presence
of smoke.

II—AGRICULTURAL MID-WEST

Over the great rolling prairies of the Middle West—a terrain
so vast that it sweeps past mere geographical limits, impinges
on the East, rolls over into the South, reaches out into the
West—there unfolds an enormous panorama of agriculture in
its myriad of outward forms. In the easterly part of this
region you look at a carpet of lightly woven patterns, with
green predominating in every known shade, many patches of
light brown and yellow where a crop has been harvested, and
here and there the dark-brown squares of a field newly plowed.
Farms of a few hundred acres appear small from the air when
you look in any given direction and see more than fifty miles
of land, literally hundreds of square miles of it, reaching out

from under the plane and losing itself to sight in the dim distance. Now a yellow cornfield, then a great splash of sugar-beet tops; on the left a brilliant green meadow, on the right a copse—seemingly forever nature at its most kaleidoscopic; for as you wing your way swiftly across this landscape the patterns seem always to be moving and falling into new places.

Monotonous? Yes, and yet the monotony is broken ever and again by some mighty river, such as the Missouri or the Mississippi, writhing its way over the face of this broad farming country; or by a town proudly rearing itself above the tranquillity of the countryside and puffing clouds of smoke as if to show its superiority. Always there are roads, some white, some gray and some almost an ebony black; some curving, some crooked and some so straight that your eye may follow them perhaps for sixty or more miles until the whiteness of their surfaces narrows to a thread of cotton and disappears close to where the blue begins. Railroads, too, abound, their permanent ways a deep brown or a coal black, but aglitter where the sun's rays light up the cold steel. Every so often there is a farmhouse or a cluster of houses marking brilliantly some picturesque village or drably some prosaic hamlet, treeless and gloomy. But even here distance lends enchantment to the eye, and the sorriest of small towns may look spotless and white.

Chicago has long vaunted its superiority as the greatest railroad center in the world. A view of this mid-Western metropolis fully justifies its pretensions. From every side the railroads run into the middle of the city. A thin, straggling

line coalesces with another and then with another, and all
form a broad track of innumerable parallel lines burying themselves in the heart of a district of massed buildings.   The iron
highways from the East and the West ride boldly through the
city, making a magnificent sweep here and spraying out into
a fork there, cleaving the town into two indistinct halves.
Down from the North comes another steel artery to weave
its lines into the gigantic network.   In a dozen places great
railroad yards spread out, sometimes almost bare, often packed
with cars from the four corners of the country, while a herd
of iron horses is to be seen snorting smoke and steam.

Here is a city at its hugest.   It will take you somewhere
near a quarter of an hour to fly across it from Lake Michigan
to the north side across the downtown section, with its teem-
ing Loop, out across a forest of smokestacks and on over a
straggling nondescript area, partly residential, partly business, and partly industrial.   It is an ugly city from the air, a
city which seems to have sacrificed itself entirely to Mammon.
But it has its finer points.   It has a superb skyline, outmatched
only by that of Manhattan and San Francisco, built on a hill.
In the Loop district many a tall building soars upward with a
beauty in graphic relief from the squalidness of its background.
It is made the more beautiful by the wide apron of water that
is seen in front.

To the eastward stretches Lake Shore Drive with its fringe
of fine residences and its thin stream of green.   Seen basked
in the golden light of the setting sun Chicago presents one of
the most impressive sights of civilization to be seen from the

air, certainly the most impressive in the Middle West, for the shadows hide much of its unsightliness and the soft light shows up its more prominent features in a harmonious relief. But at other times Chicago presents anything but harmony—an incongruous, sprawling wilderness of stark efficiency at its starkest.

III—THE GREAT PLAINS

There is no clear-cut boundary line between the Middle West and the area of the Great Plains. You first become conscious of a change in the patterns on the ground through a growth in their size. The farther west you fly, the larger the fields get. Presently there are no fields, except an isolated one here and there striving to keep up appearances. Fences and hedges are gone. Trees are sparse, and they, too, finally disappear. A farmhouse is rare. There is almost nothing but miles of sage brush and unrestricted grazing land, trailing off south into sweltering desert, which would take you days to cross on foot, and halted at the north by the sentrylike peaks of the lower Rockies, which seem to forbid the plains to pass. Here is the Great Plains region expressing our boundlessness, freely and effectively.

A herd of horses stampedes madly as the plane is heard roaring in the sky. You can see them gallop for half a mile and turn around to look for the enemy. Seeing none, they go on eating, somewhat stupidly. A little further along you may see a magnificent herd of steers, several hundred of them, dots of roan on an arid background, burned brown in August, over much of which only the intertwining cowpaths are to be seen.

But cattle are more placid than horses, and they take no notice of the noise in the heavens. There are no roads, except a dusty thin highway, which you glimpse from time to time. A railroad bed spans the land, camouflaging itself neatly in the color scheme. These are the only signs of civilization over great stretches of this terrain, and somehow they seem strangely incongruous in the wide open spaces.

On the Great Plains proper there are no cities, only cities dwarfed to raw western towns. In contrast with the East and the Middle West, where towns and cities are frequent, even a raw town is met with only every hundred miles or so, or so it seems. One sees a cluster of buildings, most of them of wood, with Main Street almost crying out from its midst. Then, a couple of hundred miles further to the west, you find surrounded by a great stock country, a sparse, gaunt-looking terrain, and like a dot on its face, a large settlement. Involuntarily one's mind springs to cowboys and wooden sidewalks. Seen from the air there is nothing even pretty about it; it is about as drab as the countryside surrounding it, only a little more matter of fact, a little more ordered. But there is an emphatic mark of modernity—a little airport nestling close to its side.

IV—Mountains of the West

Where grandeur and enchantment play hide and seek is in the mountains of the West. Here are sights reserved for the gods, which it is becoming man's privilege to see as the gods are supposed to see them. Perhaps the most enchanting area is between Cheyenne and Salt Lake City, over the Laramie

Range, across the Red Desert and over the Wasatch Mountains. This, the Cordilleran region, is famous country, scene of many a bitter fight and many a long day's trek by the pioneers of the covered wagon and Pony Express.   Close to the Colorado borderline the plane carries you through a pass in the southern tip of the Laramie Mountains, and before you stretches a broad valley, bounded by mountains.   The valley is no ordinary one.   Its distinguishing feature is the number of lakes which dot it.   There are literally hundreds of them, some of them no more than mere puddles, some a mile or more across. This is the sheep country.

You now begin to cross the Great Divide.   Contrary to expectations there are no mountains in the immediate path of flight.   You do not climb upward and top a great range, one side sweeping west and one sweeping east.   The Divide is marked by nothing more romantic than an undrained valley. It is broader than it is long, being about 100 miles across from east to west and about 60 miles from north to south, making its position as a continental divide an extraordinary anomaly.

Once across this valley the plane nears the Red Desert.   Here is an area mottled by sage brush.   The mountains fade into the distance.   Every now and then an odd piece of tesselated rock juts up from the level of the ground and finally rises on the south into a long stratalike cliff running to the west for miles.   On the left you pass a gigantic natural amphitheatre looking for all the world like nature's replica of the Yale Bowl, formed by a series of ridged hills encircling a small basin. For miles there is nothing but almost bare ground, bleak,

dismal.   Not a house as far as the eye can see.   A wilderness
where man and his works are dwarfed by immensity.

Slowly, almost imperceptibly, the landscape begins to grow
red.   The fringe of the Red Desert has been reached.   But
although it begins to be red, this great desert never seems to
achieve enough of that coloring to justify its name.   There
are too many other colors and none is at all times evident.
Allow your eyes to sweep the countryside and it is as dull and
drab as ever, except for the vermilion-streaked cliffs in the
south.   Look at it closer and you begin to see all shades of
red—brick red, russet red and vermilion.   Large stretches
are gray and brown, with here and there a dusty green patch,
enlivened every so often by a brilliant dash of purple or yellow.   A solitary road, its bed a deep russet red, now winds itself
into sight from the north and runs for miles parallel with the
line of flight.

Further along is Rock Springs, a gold-mining center, a desolate place, hardly relieved by the red embankments which
have been thrown up to provide a railroad to a plainly visible
mine shaft.   But before you reach these your plane carries
you over innumerable dunes, some of them a hundred or more
feet high, great hillocks of sand that are continually on the
move, driven by the winds which sweep from the distant mountains and down along the desert.   Nature is rarely so grandiose.

But go on over the mountains beyond the dusty desert of
Nevada, on high over the Sierras, on over wooded hills hundreds of miles square.   We come to San Francisco, standing
at the Golden Gate.   If it be early in the morning the Bay is

quiet, except for a few ferries plowing their way between the
metropolis and the mainland. To the north and to the south
and to the east the land rises in a series of rugged hills sweeping up in the early morning mist into the foothills of the Nevada
Sierras. To the west, past the Golden Gate, lies the shrouded
Pacific. Here, indeed, is a gateway to a great beyond, unfath-
omable and yet alluring. The great ocean spreads into the
dim distance and melts some twenty miles or so away into
where the water and the sea mist and the blue sky confuse
themselves into a sun-shot horizon.

Fly north from San Francisco to Seattle and you pass over
almost endless ranges of thickly forested hills. Hills? Really
mountains, several thousand feet high, but hills, nevertheless,
compared with the giant peaks you see rearing their snowy
heads high through the clouds. There are times when as
far as you can see there is nothing but forest, dark green fir
and pine, with the rock of a mountain side falling away a sheer
thousand feet or so—a contrast so sharp that you are reminded
that beneath the dipping irregular tree tops (a rough sea of
green, the waves lapping gently here and surging up madly
in other places) is Mother Earth. But this vast sea of trees
is only an illusion. Between the plane and those far-off trees
on a high hill lies a valley.

There are endless valleys, long stretches of cultivated ground
dotted here and there by a village or town and almost always
threaded by a winding river. There are times in flying over
this mountainous country when you gaze on the ground as if
from some rocky eminence instead of from an airplane wing-

ing its way at 100 miles an hour some 6,000 or 8,000 feet above
sea level; for actually the plane is flying so low, frequently
through mountain passes, that the land on either side of you
sweeps upward and higher than the altitude at which you are
flying.

After the plane has proceeded up the Sacramento Valley,
one of the most beautiful sights to be seen lies in Oregon, not
far away from the California border. To the east, perhaps
thirty miles away, but clearly visible in their crystal magnifi-
cence, jut three snow-capped peaks—the Three Sisters, each
about two miles high, mothers of the Cascade Range. A few
hours later you cross one of the most clearly marked state
boundaries in the country, where the wide Columbia River
cleaves its way between Oregon and Washington. Soon, if
you are alert, you will see shimmering in the distance a white
sun-caught glacier, lying like a blanket on the side of Mount
Rainier, a peak which darts up into the sky nearly three miles
above sea level. There is not a more inspiring sight in the
whole of this sometimes wild region than this gigantic mountain, the third highest in the continental United States, but
ninety-three feet lower than the highest, Mount Whitney,
snow-white lord of the Sierras, in Northern California.

No one passenger in a single air trip can hope to see all there
is to be seen or to describe it accurately. There are only the
high lights which impress themselves indelibly on the mind—
only the spirit of a vast country caught here and there in its
many moods—the rest, the detail, escapes.

AROUND THE WORLD BY AIRSHIP

BY WILBUR R. HANAWALT

THE 'round-the-world flight of the *Graf Zeppelin*, which started and ended at Lakehurst, New Jersey, and the itinerary of which lay across the Atlantic, Europe, Asia, the Pacific and the United States, marked the start of a new and potent phase of international understanding and co-operation. For its successful completion, the flight required the unselfish co-operation of all those nations in the Northern Hemisphere over which it passed. This great aeronautical achievement aroused the friendly admiration of all peoples of the world, but especially those of the countries in which it made stops. It centered the attention and enlisted the sympathies of the peoples of the earth on an endeavor that erased international lines and international differences.

Dr. Hugo Eckener, commander of the *Graf Zeppelin*, took off from Lakehurst, New Jersey, on August 8th on the world flight, after the ship had received careful preparation for the flight. Its 3,708,000 cubic feet of hydrogen gas was checked, the hull over its entire 776-foot length was inspected carefully, as were the five engines which, with a total of 2,550 horsepower, gave the craft its speed. There were sixty-one persons aboard—twenty passengers and a crew of forty-one. Among the passengers was

Commander Charles E. Rosendahl, commander of the Naval Air Station at Lakehurst. The crossing of the Atlantic was made in a new record time; the ship reached the coast of Europe in 44 hours, and her home base at Friedrichshafen in 55½ hours, having bettered her former time of 72 hours, and having covered a distance of 4,200 miles. On this first leg of the journey, the *Graf Zeppelin* headed straight east for the first 1,000 miles to evade a storm centered in Canada, then had favorable weather on the remainder of the crossing with a 40-mile tail wind which increased the speed of the craft to 105 miles an hour.

In Germany the *Graf* was again checked and the engines, after the installation of a valve spring and spark plug, were in condition to continue the flight. On August 15th the ship started on her second hop, Friedrichshafen to Tokio, a distance of 7,000 miles over territory unmapped and unexplored. The estimated time for the distance to Tokio was 120 hours, and the longest former flight of the Zeppelin had been 111 hours. There was no meteorological or weather report available on the vast distances of the Siberian waste, and although all European observers and two Russian organizations, the Osoaviakim and the Soviet Radio Association, arranging to work in day and night shifts to keep in touch with the Zeppelin, contributed to Dr. Eckener's knowledge of weather possibilities over the territory, his data was incomplete.

The craft loaded supplies for 150 hours and set out to fly over Berlin, Danzig, the steppes, the Siberian tundra and the Asiatic mountains. The rather sketchy weather map made from insufficient data by Dr. Eckener and Dr. Seilkopf, the weather expert on board, turned out to be correct. The weather on the flight was favorable; fortune and skill aided the German commander. With favoring weather the ship maintained an average speed of about 64 miles an hour on the long flight. Over the last 600 miles of her journey the dirigible ran into a fog which required a change in her course. After leaving Siberia behind, she flew down the west coast of Hokkaido, the northernmost of the main islands of the Japanese group, and after covering the 6,955-mile flight in 101 hours and 53 minutes, arrived in Tokio on August 19th.

The people of Japan welcomed the international adventurer with an enthusiasm equal to that which the Western Hemisphere had displayed; the factories of the nation blasted their whistles in welcome, the crowds cheered, the band played the German national anthem, and eight planes escorted the Zeppelin to the Kasumigaura Airport, forty miles northeast of Tokio. The passengers and crew of the ship were feted by the Japanese officials. The inspection of the engines again showed that they had withstood the rigors of the flight across the Atlantic, Europe and Asia without impairing their efficiency. One hundred Japanese naval mechanics worked on the ship while searchlights and all facilities of the Japanese navy aided the preparations of the craft for the continuation of its voyage; 950,000 cubic feet of hydrogen and pyrofax combined for fuel was loaded, and the lifting gas of the ship increased.

Dr. Eckener plotted his next flight straight for Los Angeles, spurning the possibility of remaining near land by following the course over the Aleutian Islands. The Japanese Weather Bureau made a complete survey of the whole western Pacific area, showing a favorable report.   The ship's route lay over the great circle, 200 miles south of land, and along the steamer lanes from Yokohama to Seattle and Vancouver.   Shortly after the take-off on August 23d, storm areas were reported northeast of Japan over the Aleutian Islands and the Bering Sea, creating a hazard along the great circle route.   Three hours out of Japan the storm hit the airship, and without a moment's hesitation, the *Graf Zeppelin's* commander ordered a change in direction straight into the spaces of the Pacific along a route 500 miles to the south of the intended course, to evade the storm area.   The ship encountered wind and rain, but she rode through the squall into clear weather.   Reports from the United States Weather Bureau aided the commander in shifting his course to a favorable route. All facilities of the American Army and Navy, by official order, were utilized for sending meteorological communications to the *Graf Zeppelin* on her Pacific crossing.   Schedules were made for communication every four hours.   The Zeppelin passed over the Golden Gate at San Francisco on August 25th, and after circling that city, proceeded to Los Angeles where she completed the third section of her 'round-the-world trip on August 26th, having covered 5,800 miles in 78 hours and 58 minutes.

Two thousand four hundred miles of airline distance remained for the completion of the flight.   The Transcontinental Air Transport offered the use of its lighted airway and meteorological services for the flight across the United States.   Seven of the crew were sent by plane to New York in order that the ship might carry more mail, and to facilitate the crossing of the Rocky

The Graf Zeppelin over Lower New York City after Its Trip Around the World, Accomplished in 21 Days

Mountains, considered one of the most dangerous parts of the world tour.   In Arizona headwinds were encountered, necessitating a change of course.   The ship headed for Fort Worth from El Paso, then followed a northerly route over Chicago, Detroit and Cleveland.

While crossing the United States the dirigible's wireless operator was in constant communication with the ground, receiving communications and reports.   Throughout the entire world flight the wireless operator kept in constant touch with the world, and received all available data to aid the selection of routes.   This performance proved the high safety factor that is given to a dirigible by its ability to use wireless efficiently.

The *Graf Zeppelin* came to earth at Lakehurst on August 29th, after having traveled a distance of 19,000 miles around the world in 21 days, 7 hours and 34 minutes.   The route taken from Los Angeles covered 2,940 miles, which required 51 hours.   The flight had been a dramatic exposition of man's mechanical advance in one branch of aeronautics.   It had also revealed some requirements of the dirigible which have not yet been supplied.   It showed that mechanical means of handling airships will be required for dirigible service of any degree of efficiency, as will be improved sheds and terminal facilities, better weather information, and larger and speedier airships.

From the cabin of the Zeppelin, Commander Eckener stepped into a round of banquets and celebrations.   He went to Washington to receive President Hoover's congratulations with those of other government officials.   Returning to New York, he received the city's welcome, and, after seeing the *Graf Zeppelin* start on her flight home to Friedrichshafen, he visited the National Air Races at Cleveland. He then proceeded to Akron to confer with officials of the Goodyear-Zeppelin Corporation concerning the establishment of dirigible services.

Two trans-oceanic services were planned: weekly mail and passenger service from the United States to Hawaii, later to be extended to the Orient, and service from Europe and America. The Goodyear concern will build two Zeppelins for the trans-Pacific service, and the German Zeppelin Company is planning two similar ships for the Atlantic line. The program will be carried out by an affiliation of American and German groups.

The *Graf Zeppelin*, after refueling, flew to Germany with 17 passengers under the command of Capt. Ernst A. Lehmann, assistant director of the Zeppelin Works. The flight was made in 66 hours, which made the time of the Germany to Germany 'round-the-world trip one day less than the Lakehurst to Lakehurst time. On the invitation of Dr. Eckener, three officers of the U. S. Navy made the return flight to gain experience which would aid them in operating Navy dirigibles. The officers designated to make the flight were Lieutenant Commander Herbert V. Wiley, commanding officer of the Navy dirigible, *Los Angeles;* Lieutenant Commander J. M. Shoemaker, in charge of the engine section of the Bureau of Aeronautics, and Lieutenant Roland G. Mayer, Construction Corps, attached to the *Los Angeles*.

It was especially appropriate that, as the *Graf Zeppelin* once more rested in her berth at Friedrichshafen, the weather observers of all the principal nations should be journeying to

Copenhagen to formulate plans for oceanic weather reports. If the plans of the meeting are put into effect, the recent flight will be the last made with inadequate weather-reporting facilities. Surface ships of Great Britain, France, Germany and the United States will co-operate to secure and broadcast twice daily weather reports which will make the North Atlantic safer for aerial navigation. With the additional aid of Denmark and Japan, which will probably contribute the use of their stations, information concerning the meteorological conditions of the entire Northern Hemisphere will be available to scientists in the principal flying countries. Uncharted air routes, such as confronted the *Graf Zeppelin* over Siberia and the Pacific, will soon become things of the past.

The 'round-the-world flight was significant as an achievement of aeronautics. It was the completion of dreams and a hope formed in the mind of Count Zeppelin in 1873, when he designed his first rigid airship. It proved to the public the feasibility of safe airships, and of safe aerial travel across the oceans. It confirmed the calculations of the ship's engineers and designers as to its structural strength for withstanding unfavorable weather, showed them with what forces the dirigible of the future must be able to cope, and flung out a challenge to weather observers and meteorologists to find a means of directing such aerial transports over favorable routes.

But, by engrossing the attention of all nations in a solution of common transport problems, and by calling for the unselfish co-operation of European, Asiatic and American nations, the flight of the *Graf Zeppelin* had a greater significance as a means of uniting international endeavor for a mutual cause that will result in a more intimate understanding between nations. The plans which have been formulated for trans-oceanic airship lines to be operated between continents by an international group, as a result of this flight, will advance the same cause for which the nations of the earth are now striving—the establishment of international trust for the perpetuation of peace.

PARACHUTES!

BY LIEUT. H. B. MILLER, U. S. N.
*Engineering Officer, Fighting Plane Squadron Two
Aircraft Squadrons, Battle Fleet, U. S. Navy*

IN approximately the year 1790, J. P. Blanchard, a Frenchman, first used a parachute in conjunction with a balloon. An unfortunate, and unwilling, stray dog was the first jumper, and he had to be thrown over the side of the balloon basket by the scruff of the neck. The tests were considered successful, and three years later Blanchard essayed a jump. Because his rate of descent, however, was a trifle high, he suffered a broken leg.

On October 22, 1797, Andre Jacques Garnerin made the first entirely successful parachute drop at Paris. His apparatus oscillated so violently from side to side that it was thought for a while that he would surely be thrown out of the basket, which at that time was always suspended from a parachute.

Leonardo da Vinci discussed the principles of the parachute, and mention is made of one in a book published by the Italian, Fauste de Veranzio. Again in 1691, we are told, a man proved to be the life of the party when he entertained the Court in Paris by taking huge leaps with the aid of two parachutes which were lashed to his waist.

During all this time the shape of parachutes in general remained similar to those we now possess. In the effort to develop a more stable apparatus, Robert Cocking, an Englishman, contrived a novel design. The shape was conical, as before, except that the vertex was downward. Framework supported the sides of the cone.

Apparently no stray animals were available on the evening of July 24, 1873, when Cocking ascended in a balloon from Vauxhall Gardens, London. At an altitude of 5,000 feet, he mounted his invention and cut himself free of the balloon. For a moment the descent was stable and quite normal. The strain then became too great, the parachute collapsed and sent Cocking at a terrific rate of speed to his doom.

The development of parachutes progressed slowly, and of necessity, with balloons. Balloons were even deflated in the air and parachuted to the ground; the loose fabric gathered in the top of the surrounding network formed a perfect parachute.

Before the World War, parachute jumpers were daredevils who earned a precarious livelihood by thrilling the crowds at County Fairs. The "jumps" were really ''releases'' from a free balloon. The parachute was usually secured to the hanging-bar of the balloon by a light cord. The lines, or shrouds, were secured to a harness worn by the jumper. When sufficient altitude had been reached, the performer opened the gas valve on the balloon, released his grip on the hanging-bar and fell clear. His weight was sufficient to break the cord holding the apparatus to the balloon.

The parachute generally opened immediately and lowered the

jumper to the ground, where he commandeered the first available horse and buggy to give chase to his falling, run-away balloon. He was always followed by an admiring army of small boys. His chase successful, the "death-defying aeronaut" returned to collect his salary. The more canny of the Fair treasurers never paid the balloonist before the jump because there were cases on record where the parachute had failed to open!

The advent of airplanes, however, introduced a new factor in jumping. A balloon, if it moved at all, continued to gain altitude, especially when the weight of the jumper was removed. This was an ideal condition for the jumper, since there was no danger of his 'chute fouling on the balloon. The airplane, on the other hand, was a fast moving machine, which might hit a person after he had jumped over the side. What was worse, the parachute, with its long tenuous folds, might foul some part of the plane and drag the aviator along dangling at the end of his useless 'chute.

Nevertheless, in March, 1912, Captain Bert Berry made the first jump from a plane at Jefferson Barracks, Missouri. The plane was a Benoist Pusher, piloted by Tony Jannus. The parachute was packed in a metal cone fastened under the forward part of the plane. Berry climbed down to the axle, slipped into the harness, and dropped from the plane. The jerk of the fall pulled the parachute out of its container, broke the retaining cord, and settled the adventurous captain gently down to earth.

The impetus given to aviation by the World War was astonishing, surprising no one more than the involved belligerents. But on the whole, the efforts made to put more and more planes in the air served to over-balance any efforts made to safeguard the pilots already there. War was in the air. Men had to be expended. Planes had to be built. No time was available to give to research for safety in a business that was at first looked on as exhilarating adventure.

The use of parachutes was forgotten until planes began to fly at night on bombing raids. Cities in the war zones learned their lessons rapidly and soon no lights were allowed to remain visible to the night bombers. If only cities could be illuminated for just a minute or so! Parachute flares were the result. These flares were thrown over the side of the planes. A time fuse set off the illuminating charge and released a small 'chute, which slowly lowered the lighting apparatus. This illumination helped the bombers to find their targets.

In this war, as in others, spies formed a more or less reliable means of information regarding the movements of the enemy forces. Again aviation showed the way. Secret agents were ferried across the front lines in planes and landed far into the back country. From there their spying activities began. This practice was very successful at first, but before long the irregular landing of any plane foretold a spy-hunt which resulted fatally for the agent, if discovered.

If only the landing could be eliminated! Of course, a parachute! But that could be seen as easily as a plane landing. Not at night! Thus the parachute began to lower human beings from a plane. The parachutes were made of black material and the mystery-men wore dark coveralls. Truly a ghost to come floating silently down in enemy territory at night.

The familiar captive sausage balloon was used for observing enemy movements from the beginning of the conflict. This duty for a time was comparatively safe and routine. Soon, however, the art of airplane construction advanced to a point where fighting planes, which lived up to their names, were being produced by all of the belligerents. The occupation of a balloon observer then became a precarious one, indeed. Armed with machine guns loaded with incendiary bullets, pursuit planes began the playful habit of dropping down out of the clouds upon the unsuspecting gas bags. Anchored to the ground, these elephantine objects were perfect targets, and being inflated with hydrogen, were also perfect firetraps.

Parachutes were resorted to by the observers on both sides. That application was the first utilization of this old invention as an actual life-saving device. Always before it had been a thrill-producer for people who invariably thought the parachute-jumper was slightly crazy. Perhaps, in those days, they were right.

Having no past experience upon which to base their demands, the observers adopted the parachute gear in its entirety as used on the old free-balloons. The top of the parachute was attached to the balloon basket by a cord; the other end was secured to a harness attached to the man. The observer merely jumped over the side. His weight broke the retaining cord and allowed him to float gently to earth.

Continually carrying the 'chute attached to his body proved to be a nuisance, however. The parachute shrouds were then made fast to a small metal ring. The observer wore his harness as before, but he was free from his clumsy burden. When he desired to use it, he snapped the ring on to his harness and jumped exactly as he had before.

When struck by a flaming projectile the hydrogen-filled balloons instantly took fire and exploded.   Unless the occupants were quick to jump, they would not get clear of the burning bag. If they did get clear, another danger beset them. Fragments of burning balloon fabric might fall on their cotton canopies and ignite them.   Either would be disastrous.

The result of these dangers was to make balloon observers super-sensitive to the sound of diving airplanes and the rat-tat-tat of a firing machine gun. Either was a signal to jump immediately. Men frequently jumped even at the approach of friendly aircraft when their identity was in doubt. There were even instances in which observers, in their haste to leave, failed to attach the parachute ring to their harness—and jumped!

The hazards to airplanes during this period were many. Fires in the air were common, wings often folded up during long, fast dives, and collisions were not infrequent. Always the pilot and gunner were carried helplessly down to their fate. The pilots, being only human, did not look ahead to a long or rosy future.

To Germany appears to belong the credit for first applying the parachute to heavier-than-air craft. At first each pilot made his own. Eventually each squadron began to manufacture such equipment for its own pilots, and finally the German Air Service began to supply all of its airmen with parachutes.

These safety devices were crude affairs at best. A box or

bucket was built into the plane with the opening downward. In this was piled the parachute. The harness was, of course, worn by the aviator. The theory was that the man would jump and pull his parachute out of its compartment as he went. Actually, the fabric was more than apt to foul on the plane and fail to allow the aviator to fall clear. It was better than nothing, however.

During the spring of 1918 the first successful emergency jump was made by a German flier in a Heinecke parachute. This German was patroling near the front lines at about 22,000 feet, in terrifically cold weather. Suddenly his plane burst into flames. Here was a problem to test anyone's nerves. No one had ever before been saved by deserting a moving airplane during an emergency. Should he jump and either be saved or quickly destroyed, or should he stay with his ship to await a slow fiery death? What thoughts must have flashed through the mind of that pioneer! After a few futile attempts to extinguish the inferno by side-slipping, the pilot made his momentous decision. He leaped over the side. His parachute opened immediately. His progress downward was made directly over the front lines, but at the last moment a gust of wind drifted him behind the American trenches. The German's legs were nearly frozen, and both of them had been shot by soldiers in both lines. As if the aviator had not encountered sufficient danger for one day!

The Allied Air Forces immediately adopted the balloon parachutes that appeared most practicable for their airplanes. From these the newly organized American Air Service developed two types of parachutes, which combined the best qualities of the

Allied safety devices. During the same period, the Engineering Division of the American Air Service was carrying on extensive experiments in the United States. Then the war ended.

The experiments were continued, however, at McCook Field, Dayton, Ohio. Tests were made on all the parachutes available at the close of the war. The men carrying on this work were J. M. Russell, J. J. Higgins, Floyd Smith, G. M. Ball, and Major E. L. Hoffman.

Very little data was available for these men to use in their work. The parachute designed by Charles Broadwick offered some ideas to the investigators. No one knew what quality of material was most desirable, nor the inflated shape which would give the best results. It was known, however, that it was imperative for the parachute to be manually operated; that is, when the aviator jumped from the plane, his parachute would be with him unopened until after he was entirely clear of his ship. The jumper would then operate some opening device and float to earth under the inflated 'chute.

Besides the chances of fouling on the plane when the parachute was attached to the ship, cases actually occurred in which the pilot, after jumping, traveled downward at the same speed as the plane. Hence, the parachute retaining cord was never broken free of the ship. The apparatus never had an opportunity to function.

Silk was early decided upon as the most desirable material, and Japanese habutai silk has been used almost exclusively ever since. There are several reasons for this. Its strength for its weight is great; it can be packed in a small space; it has a "springiness" which permits it to unfold and separate easily. Of vital importance is the fact that it has the ability to resist flames.

Cotton fabric can be used, and has been, successfully in a great many cases. But it deteriorates more rapidly than silk. As long as the supply of silk is plentiful and comparatively cheap, it is likely that we will continue to use it in our parachutes.

Whenever a new idea occurred to the investigators, one of the men would go up in a plane and jump, or a weighted dummy would be dropped, to prove or disprove the worth of it. The slow method of trial and error was the only practical means of progress. Nevertheless, by the latter part of 1919, a serviceable 'chute had been developed.

Several old theories had to be disproved. Mistakes in reasoning were often discovered by accident. It was formerly thought, for instance, that if a man were to fall a few hundred feet or more at a tremendous rate of speed, he would be unconscious or most certainly physically helpless. People argued that under these conditions, it would be impossible to operate a 'chute even if the man were to clear the plane. A harness failure occurred to Lieut. R. A. Caldwell of the Royal Flying Corps while making a demonstration jump, which caused him to fall 600 feet to his death. However, it did demonstrate that a man has complete possession of his faculties during a fall. Throughout the drop, Lieutenant Caldwell was observed to be searching all over the harness in an effort to discover some means of operating his parachute. To show how completely this idea has changed, the record for a delayed jump—that is, the distance from the point of departure from the plane to the point of parachute operation—is now said to be more than 9,000 feet.

It was further argued that a man could not climb clear of a plane falling or diving at a high rate of speed. In 1920 Lieutenant Patterson and an observer were sent aloft from McCook Field to test machine guns in the low temperatures found at high altitudes. Just what happened is not known, but down came the plane out of control. At about 10,000 feet the wings were torn off by the terrific velocity. Finally the tail surfaces parted and left the fuselage to hurtle down to destruction alone. In spite of the speed, one of the aviators climbed out on to the fuselage. This proved clearly that a man could escape from a fast-moving plane if only he had some means of saving himself after he succeeded in getting out. It is, indeed, unfortunate that so many men had to sacrifice their lives before certain definite facts were known.

When the jumper touches earth after a drop in a strong wind, he is apt to be dragged along the ground for some distance before he can "spill the wind" out of the 'chute, and get out of the harness. Any bruises that result from a jump invariably occur at this stage of the procedure. A quick releasing device was adopted with which to disconnect the jumper from the parachute upon landing. It consisted of a lever which was manually operated. This idea bid fair to be quite successful until three men within a very short period released themselves accidentally while still hundreds of feet in the air, with the result that this innovation was rapidly cast aside.

Various improvements and modifications resulted until parachutes reached their present form.   Various types of parachutes have been produced and offered to the air services for testing. Some have been of value; others have been far from positive in their actions.

On August 24, 1920, Mr. O'Connor was to demonstrate the Jahn parachute.   Army officials insisted that the jumper wear a service type 'chute as a reserve.   Although both Mr. O'Connor and Mr. Jahn protested vigorously against this precaution, the Army men were adamant.   The demonstrator went up and jumped from a height of 2,000 feet.   Nothing happened until he had reached a height of 500 feet.   At this point the service parachute was called into use.   It saved the demonstrator, for the new device, under test, had fouled its cordage.

The first *emergency* jump with a pack parachute took place on October 20, 1922.   Lieut. H. R. Harris of the Army was engaged in a dog fight over McCook Field.   His pursuit plane was placed in a steep bank while making 150 miles per hour.   Suddenly the wings began to vibrate severely, tearing apart internally. Lieutenant Harris quickly decided his only chance was to jump. With this in mind, he unfastened his safety belt and stood up in his seat.   He was blown from the diving plane, and after some difficulty, found the rip-cord ring which he pulled.   Although he had fallen from 2,500 to 500 feet before opening his parachute, he suffered only a few bruises.

In general, the practical use of parachutes was viewed with much suspicion and doubt by aviators.   In 1923 orders were issued to all Army and Navy fliers requiring them to wear a parachute on every flight. Most pilots, however, avoided wearing them if it were possible to take off without them. If compelled to do so, they would carry them to their planes, and then sit on them without so much as attaching the harness to themselves.

There were various reasons for this reluctance to adopt 'chutes. Few of the pilots had ever actually seen a descent, although two fliers had successfully made emergency jumps in the post-war pack 'chutes.

The new devices were far from comfortable when worn. Because the cockpits of the planes had not been designed for parachutes, it was with great difficulty that both the pilot and his 'chute could get into the same cockpit at one time.

Probably the predominant reason, and the most absurd, was one of psychology. Most pilots feared that their comrades would think they were afraid to be aloft without a safety-first appliance! That, perhaps, appears to be an impossible line of reasoning, yet consider how many of us fear what others may think of our everyday actions.

The eventual conversion of all service pilots to the every-day use of 'chutes came with faith in their ability to operate successfully in an emergency. For it was inevitable that faith should be established as more and more pilots were saved from certain death.

The first emergency jump in naval aviation was made by Gunner W. M. Cole on October 16, 1924. Cole was flying under clouds at about 1,200 feet. Suddenly he felt a shock and saw that his left wing had been carried away by a second plane which had dived through the clouds. With his ship out of control he jumped clear, counted three, and pulled his rip-cord. The parachute opened at once, and landed him on the golf course of the Coronado Country Club. The occupants of the other plane did not survive the collision.

There are two methods of using a parachute. The first is termed the "pull off." The jumper walks out on the wing to a point where the opening 'chute will not foul the tail surfaces. There he pulls the rip-cord. The 'chute fills out in the wind blast, and the jumper is pulled off the plane and out into space. This method, however, is generally impractical for emergency jumps, being restricted to the training of parachute jumpers or used for exhibition purposes.

The second manner of jumping is the "free-fall," in which the jumper dives head first from the plane, waits until he is clear and then operates his rip-cord. This is the type of jump generally used for emergencies.

The minimum altitude for an emergency jump consistent with safety is considered to be not under 400 feet. Yet Walter Lees, a civilian pilot, who was flying a German war type LVG airplane near Dayton, jumped while his ship was at an altitude of 150 feet after his controls had jammed. The rip-cord was pulled and the parachute opened immediately to give the pilot a safe landing.

To the Army goes the credit for the highest jump on record. The jumper was Captain Stevens, whose interest lies more with aerial photography than with parachutes. One day when ascending on a photographic mission, he decided to make a record jump. At 26,000 feet he waved to the pilot, stepped over the side of the plane, and made a safe landing some twenty minutes later.

Parachute jumping at air meets is generally formed into a contest.   The object is for the jumper to land as close as possible to a mark on the field.   Professionals become uncannily proficient at this sport, although things may go wrong.   The parachutist may not "slip his 'chute" accurately enough to direct his course, or the wind itself may play unexpected tricks.

Parachutes are sometimes used under unintentional circumstances.   In the summer of 1928, Lieut. Dick Gaines was practicing acrobatics in a Navy fighting plane at an altitude of 9,000 feet.   While in the inverted position at the top of a loop, he decided to fly on his back.   His control stick was pushed forward, but too far, for the plane stalled while on its back. It then whipped into the mysterious "outside spin" and after two dizzy turns threw Gaines out in spite of his safety belt. After an interval the astonished pilot pulled his rip-cord and floated slowly down to the surface of San Diego Bay, where he was picked up by a seaplane.

Parachutes are now in approximately the same status in commercial aviation as they were in military aviation several years ago.   Pilots who have seen lives saved generally are enthusiastic about them and some of them wear parachutes, but the percentage is pitifully small.

A year ago few, if any, commercial aviation schools used parachutes for either instructors or students.   In three cases, school operators have told representatives of a well-known parachute company that if any one school could be persuaded to use parachutes they would gladly follow the example. Here, again, responsible men were afraid of the opinion of others. Afraid to use a recognized life-saving device for fear they would be thought cowards!

Finally, a long-established aeronautical school was prevailed upon to adopt the 'chute. Furthermore, it advertised the fact. As a result, more and more operators are noticeably falling into line and installing parachutes as standard equipment.

Very few, if any, passenger planes carry parachutes for either the passengers or pilots. A well-known California operator recently stated that only a very few of his passengers asked if they were to use parachutes during a flight. After ten years, this flier has never encountered anyone who refused to take a flight because of not being equipped with one.

Would the average man or woman continue to fly with aerial transportation companies if he or she were asked to wear parachutes? Very likely not. The prospective passenger would think that the company doubted the ability of its pilots to get their planes safely back to earth. Instead, this potential passenger would go next door and fly with a company which could not afford to provide him with a last-resort safety device! Patrons of steamship companies continue to patronize ships on which life preservers are provided, for they realize that the company, instead of indicating doubt in its crews and equipment, is being foresighted.

On the other hand, there are several practical reasons why commercial transport planes do not use the parachute in its present form. Unquestionably, there are people who would not jump under any conditions. It is doubtful if an elderly person or a child would go over the side into space, even if told that it was his only chance for safety. The passenger would not know exactly when to jump. If he should become terrified by a particularly bumpy flight, he might jump a perfectly safe plane at any time.

One can picture a group of passengers being lectured to on the operation of a parachute prior to a flight. Shortly after the lecturer had come to the words, "Jump, count three and pull the ring," he would need lecture no further, for his passengers would most probably have disappeared.

It seems, then, that for passenger-carrying planes the parachute must be developed in a different direction. One method would be to drop the passenger automatically out of the plane as he sits in his seat. The parachute would, of course, function automatically. If some means could be found to lower the entire plane to safety, the element of responsibility would be removed from inexperienced passengers to a competent pilot. The pilot's technical knowledge alone would decide upon the necessity of using the safety apparatus.

The first successful drop of an airplane by means of a parachute occurred on August 24, 1926, at Inglewood, California. The plane was a war-time Jenny, weighing 2,400 pounds, and was piloted by Carl Oelze, a naval aviator. The plane was placed into a stalled position and the huge parachute was successfully operated at an altitude of 1,800 feet. Since then, several airplane drops have been made with varying degrees of success. The landing gear may be broken, but this will contribute towards relieving the shock of landing.

Parachute companies are prepared to provide any size parachute needed. Development must now come from aircraft manufacturers in the proper construction of planes strong enough to withstand the drop. The location of the parachute in the plane is an important factor in order to prevent fouling during a spin or some abnormal attitude.

A pilot does not always wait until an emergency in order to make use of his parachute. Any number of circumstances may determine its use. If engine failure occurred while flying at night over strange territory, most experienced pilots would "bail out" without hesitation rather than attempt a landing, even with special flares and landing lights. Fortunately, most airplane engines of today are reliable and this circumstance seldom happens.

The same problem is presented to the flier up over a layer of clouds or fog. It will be recalled that two of Colonel Lindbergh's four jumps resulted from arriving at his destination at night, short of gas, only to find it fog-bound. Unable to find a hole through which to descend, he climbed high just before his gas ran dry—and jumped!

The parachute is not always used as a life-saving device, though that is its primary purpose and the principal reason for its existence. It has been used as a means of getting to the ground when there was no other way possible, or when speed was desirable. In July, 1919, the British dirigible R-34 made its memorable transatlantic flight to the United States. After the ship had been buffeted about by storms and head winds, it became a grave question as to whether or not she would have sufficient fuel

to enable her to reach American shores. With economical
operation, however, the giant airship managed to reach her
destination, Long Island. A quick landing was imperative
because of the fuel shortage. In order to direct and speed up
operations, Major Pritchard descended to the ground in a
parachute. The ground forces were thus able to co-operate
more closely with those aboard the dirigible, and a landing was
speedily effected.

Everyone remembers that the Junker monoplane *Bremen*
was stranded on Greenly Island in April, 1928, after completing
the first non-stop crossing of the Atlantic by a plane from east to
west. After the pilots had been flown to New York by commercial planes, the Army undertook the job of delivering a Junker's
pilot to the *Bremen*. He was to repair the damaged plane and
fly it to New York City. General Fechet and Lieutenant
Quesada flew north in one amphibian, while Captain Eaker and
Fred Melchoir, the German pilot, flew in a second amphibian.
After numerous harrowing experiences in fog and ice, the two
Army planes reached their destination on May 19, 1928. The
winter's ice was beginning to break up and a landing on either
land or water was out of the question. Nothing daunted,
Melchior jumped with his parachute and made a safe landing
close to the *Bremen*.

The members of the Caterpillar Club are recognized as those
whose lives have been saved by an emergency jump with a parachute. Several men are double members, but Colonel Lindbergh
has the unusual distinction of having four emergency jumps to his
record. The club name is a silent tribute to the lowly creature

who spends his time weaving silk fibres which later become so vitally important to the aviator.

The parachute is not a panacea for all the deplorable accidents that happen and are bound to happen to airplanes as long as the human element enters into their operation. It offers, however, a chance to the flier when he needs it most of all. If properly used, it will operate without fail. For military pilots it is an absolute necessity.   Its use is increasing in commercial aviation and when sufficient development has taken place, its use, in some form or other, will unquestionably be universal.

FLIRTING WITH DEATH IN A PARACHUTE

BY LAUREN D. LYMAN

*Stirring Tales of Aviators Who Have Jumped from Their Planes
and Thereby Joined the Caterpillar Club*

IN the whole drama-packed history of aviation there is no chapter so filled with exciting incident, life and death action and thrills as that which tells the story of the silken parachute. The lowly silkworm, nibbling away on its mulberry leaf, has received striking tribute from the men who have saved their lives by means of the parachute, and who have banded themselves together in the famous Caterpillar Club.

There are nearly 400 of them now and every one can tell a story of high adventure and quick thinking in vital crises. The parachute is much older than aviation. It was experimented with hundreds of years ago, but it was not until the development of the heavier-than-air flying machine that its possibilities came to be recognized. There is romance in the lifeboat swinging to its davits, but the lifeboat is like any other small watercraft, whose use except on special occasions is a matter of ordinary moment. The use of the parachute in sport is exciting. But the parachute's important duty is that of protecting the lives of fliers on more than usually hazardous missions, such as flying the night mail, performing intricate military maneuvers and doing the highly necessary work of testing new machines.

By far the greater number of those who wear the golden caterpillar earned the insignia in test work and battle maneuver. Lieutenant Stephen A. McClellan of the U. S. Marine Corps was testing a new experimental pursuit plane for the marines at Anacostia one spring morning. He intended to find out the ultimate strain it would stand—to put it to such extreme tests that vital weaknesses, should there be any, would develop during the flight. After that the engineers might remedy them before the type was turned over for service.

So McClellan went up. He was equipped with a special back-type parachute pack, that is, his parachute was folded tightly into a rectangular package just the size of the back of the seat in his plane. It was strapped and buckled about his shoulders and thighs with a harness resembling that of the ordinary infantryman's pack, but heavier. At his left side, inserted into the canvas covering of the parachute, was a metal ring about six inches in diameter to which was fastened the "rip-cord" for releasing the parachute.

The pilot climbed his experimental fighter to 6,000 feet. He circled about for a few minutes, testing the sensitiveness of his controls, learning the "feel" of his craft in flight. Then pointing the nose downward, he gave his 500-horsepower motor full throttle. He was in a full power dive going straight down. From 100 his speed immediately increased to 200 miles an hour and then leaped past the 300-mile mark—more than five miles a minute—to 440 feet a second. The forces

set up by this power dive are almost beyond imagination—
a ton and a half of steel and wood and fabric held together
by slender steel cables and tubular struts, hurtling earthward
under the combined agency of gravity and the bore through
the air of an eight-foot metal blade turning at more than 2,000
revolutions a minute. Somewhere in that breath-taking dive
McClellan proposed to pull back on his stick, move the elevator
upward and come out of the dive. If the plane stood the
shock of that turn, something at least could be said for its
sturdiness. But on this occasion the pilot never had a chance
to make the test. Halfway to the ground the machine's wings
and tail came off, leaving the diving fuselage pulled earthward
by the roaring propeller.

There remained also the center section of the wing just above
the cockpit, and this broken bit was driven by the force of
the wind down over the flier's head. To get out he had to
force this section upward, which he did by exerting all of his
strength. The air slipping past at three times hurricane speed
tore it away as McClellan pushed. Next he had to get up into
this mighty blast himself. He knew the danger. He knew
that there was no time to waste. Quickly he snapped the
catch on the safety belt that held him to his seat. Then he
crouched as low as possible for a spring upward. He knew
that if on the first attempt he did not clear the cockpit and
the headrest, his chances were good in that wind for breaking
his back against the top of the cockpit.

He sprang upward. The wind caught him and snatched
him clear of the diving plane. He seized the ring, pulled the

rip-cord and the 'chute opened, jerking him upright in the harness. He had just time to realize that he was safe, for the moment at least, to look downward and see what was left of his plane strike and tear a hole in the hard ground and then to reconsider his own plight. Below him were the waters of the Anacostia River, with cakes of ice floating along. McClellan pulled down the shrouds on one side to "spill air" and slipped his parachute away from the river. He was not successful and landed with a splash in the icy waters. His predicament had been seen, however, and he was quickly rescued. He now wears the golden caterpillar.

Sometimes a flier has been thrown clear of his plane without the least intent on his part. This was the experience of Lieutenant F. O. (Tex) Rogers, also a Marine Corps test pilot, now a Captain attached to the Bureau of Aeronautics in Washington. Tex was flying along one day, at 2,500 feet, over Langley Field, Va. He decided to find out what time it was. So he unfastened his safety belt and through a pocket hole in his heavy flying suit fished for his watch. Tex is not clear to this day as to exactly what happened. One side of the belt which is attached to the underside of the pilot's seat fell to the floor of the cockpit. Rogers reached down to get it. The little fighting plane struck a bump, lurched terrifically and Rogers found himself in the air. By the bump he was catapulted clear of the plane. He fell two hundred feet before pulling the rip-cord. He landed safely near Langley Field, and the plane, its engine almost full on, flew about for a bit, then crashed some distance away.

"And I don't even remember what time it was when I looked at my watch," Tex says now in recalling his adventure.

Lieutenant James H. Doolittle, considered by many as the best pilot in the United States Army Air Service, went along for years racing planes whose safety factors were reduced to the lowest possible mark, testing all manner of experimental craft and doing stunts in the air which apparently he alone can do without serious accident. Once when his two broken ankles were in plaster casts he flew a Hawk fighter across the Andes in bad weather. Recently he landed at night in the fog a plane minus its lower wing. He had torn the wing off in a tree-top. He circled again in the monoplane he had created out of a biplane and then landed, hitting the same tree. The plane was pretty well battered, but it is flying again. Doolittle was unhurt. Last September he joined the Caterpillar Club.

"The honor was appreciated, but most unexpected," Doolittle says.

Doolittle had borrowed at the National Air Races one of the new Army fighters equipped with a 600-horsepower chemically cooled engine. He intended to try out the plane, with which he was unfamiliar, and then join Lieutenant Al Williams of the Navy in stunting exhibitions at the Air Races. Doolittle flew about five miles away from the air meet, which was at the Cleveland airport. There, over farming country, he proceeded to put the fleet little fighter through its paces as only Doolittle can. The record states that while diving at 200 miles an hour in a position "thirty degrees past the vertical," the wings came off. Doolittle himself tells little more than that. It is said, however, that he was completing his last of several outside loops when he lost his wings. In compliance with War Department orders requiring "a complete and accurate account of the causes of the emergency jump," the Lieutenant filed this statement in the office of the Chief of the Air Corps: "Wings broke." Ordered to write a "description of the method of leaving aircraft," he wrote: "Thrown out."

The picture is there in those four words. A tiny fighting plane diving upside down, the pilot hanging on his straps head downward; centrifugal force acting powerfully to tear him loose from his cockpit. Then the "wings broke," and the flier, unbuckling his belt, shot out like a bullet.

Doolittle must have been a little dazed. He pulled the ring but he did not pull it hard enough, and at first the 'chute did not open. He was tumbling downward, over and over like a whirling ball. He wrenched again and the silken folds straightened out. The straps on his shoulders and thighs jerked him violently upright.

In another hour Doolittle was again in the air in his second borrowed fighter that day, thrilling the crowds with his loops and barrel rolls and dives.

Major Horace M. Hickam, now attached to the General Staff in Washington, collided with another plane during a formation attack exercise with bombers at Langley Field. He dived and was coming up under a bomber when the plane crashed into his lower right wing, tearing out the rear strut and folding up the spar. He tried his controls and found them inoperative.

Hickam's escape was miraculous. For a second his plane was on an even keel. He unfastened his safety belt and prepared to climb out "with the birdies." His plane suddenly whip-stalled and started straight down. He was deluged with the contents of his crushed gasoline tank. He got one foot in his seat, and with hands on the sides of the cockpit pushed himself out with all his strength, then smashed straight into the tail group, caromed off and into the air. He has no recollection of pulling the rip-cord to release the 'chute.

"I immediately tried to kick loose from the wreckage and found myself sitting up in my seat with the parachute completely open. Between my knees I then watched my plane spin and crash. I remember having some faint curiosity at the time as to just how I happened to be sitting in the parachute without pulling the release ring."

At McCook Field, in Dayton, former engineering and research headquarters of the Air Corps, Lieutenant James T. Hutchinson and Observer Paul Stanley escaped by the parachute route at 8,000 feet by jumping from a burning bomber carrying six bombs, 2,000 rounds of machine-gun ammunition and 320 gallons of high-test gasoline. Hutchinson by his coolness and presence of mind probably saved the lives of several citizens of Dayton, toward the most thickly populated part of which the plane was headed when it caught fire.

Startled by a violent explosion in the engine compartment, he saw the fire wall between himself and the engine burst back-

"*Where's the pilot, Bill?*"

"*He'll be along later; he's in a parachute.*"

ward. The top cowling blew free, and at once flames filled
the cockpit and curled up about the two aviators. The entire
nose was on fire. The flames were creeping quickly toward
the gasoline and bombs. Hutchinson told Stanley to jump.
He jumped from the cockpit, struck the edge of the wing, hung
there for a moment and then shot off into space. He tumbled
over and over several times and then his 'chute opened. Hutchinson had climbed to the lower wing, stood for a moment cling-
ing to the wires and, as he said in his report, "collecting my
thoughts."

The plane was headed along a path that would have brought
it directly into the city. That flaming bomb load landing
in a street would have caused real disaster. Hutchinson
thought of this and calmly edged himself along the wing and
back to the burning cockpit. He reached through the flames
and retarded the throttle. The nose of the plane dropped
and it started downward in a steep spiral. He could not reach
the switches without thrusting his head directly into the hottest
part of the fire. Then he crawled out on the wing again and
jumped. The plane spiraled about him as he fell, and after
the parachute opened the speed of the man and the burning
machine earthward was about the same. For nearly a mile
Hutchinson and his flying fire kept pace with each other, so
close at times that the pilot feared for his life. At about 4,000
feet the plane nosed downward at a steeper angle and left
him. It burst on striking the ground.

It is one thing to jump in the daytime when the jumper can
see the ground and aid himself to some extent in landing. But

it is to the night fliers—the men who carry the mail in all sorts of weather across the Alleghenies, over rough New England and through the passes of the Rockies—that the parachute has become invaluable. As a matter of fact, parachutes were used from planes at night before they were ever adopted as a safety device. During the war spies were landed in darkness behind the German lines by the parachute route. These were war heroes whom the correspondents in their dispatches could say little about.

Colonel Charles A. Lindbergh, four times a member of the Caterpillar Club, made his third and fourth jumps from mail planes at night. Once, between St. Louis and Chicago, he found himself somewhere near his destination, Maywood Field, with a 1,000-foot fog blanket separating him from the ground. Gasoline fires and searchlights could not pierce this gloom and Lindbergh turned westward and south to get away from Lake Michigan. He flew until his gasoline was almost gone, and then climbed to 5,000 feet. Above the sky was clear. Beneath was still the fog. His engine sputtered and quit and he went over the side. Then came some mad seconds. The falling flier saw his plane coming toward him out of the darkness in a wide curve. It passed 300 yards away. Lindbergh tried to direct the course of his fall by slipping his 'chute away from the path of the derelict plane. Soon it reappeared, but not quite so close. Five times in all, this wandering plane circled into sight out of the night and disappeared again. At 1,000 feet Lindbergh went into the fog, which persisted right down to the ground. He landed easily in a cornfield.

A few months later he was caught in a snowstorm at night and with the clouds piled up in front of him to 14,000 feet. He could get neither over nor under them, and when his tanks went dry he jumped at 13,000 feet. Closer to the ground the snow had turned to rain. Lindbergh landed on top of a barbed wire fence but, owing to his heavy flying suit, he received no injury.

These are a few of the little incidents in the tale of the parachute. The history is growing month by month and will continue to grow as long as fliers and engineers persist in pioneering, or until some substitute has been found for test flying. The lives of the men who have jumped are only a few of the lives being saved daily by the parachute. It has made possible the testing of planes for inherent and secret weaknesses which perhaps would otherwise never have come to light until some fatal accident disclosed them. It is helping tremendously in the scientific attack on the mysteries of the spin which has cost so many lives, and it is making student training safer than it ever has been in the past. No reputable flying school today sends up its students without parachutes, and even the private flier in the tested and licensed plane is beginning to wear the pack wherever he goes in the skies.

SAFETY IN THE AIR

BY HARRY F. GUGGENHEIM

President Daniel Guggenheim Fund for the Promotion of Aeronautics

SOME extraordinary developments are now taking place in airplane construction. From these developments one is justified in the faith that airplanes will be produced in the not distant future which will be operated with an ease comparable to that of operating a motor car and which will offer the safest means of rapid transport in the hands of pilots even without long training and experience.

There are two kinds of passenger flying into which aviation is very surely and rapidly dividing itself. In the first place, we have passenger flying over regularly scheduled routes with best modern planes equipped with several engines and supported by a highly developed organization. This is directly analogous to passenger transportation by railroad or steamship, and it is fair to say that today, under the right conditions, this kind of air transport at least equals in safety rail and ship transport. For example, in the past three years in England regular passenger services have flown 3,200,000 miles, carrying 89,000 passengers without a single accident resulting in the injury or death of a passenger. The recent accident that

104

took place in England, causing much public notice and sympathy, occurred in an airplane which was forced down over the channel, necessitating a landing on the sea in a landplane equipped for this purpose. In addition, this was a type of plane which, although equipped with two engines, was unable to fly with its load with one engine disabled. This is an exception from the modern equipment almost exclusively used by the Imperial Airways of England. Two of what I consider the present-day seven cardinal principles of safe passenger air transport, which will be mentioned later, were not observed; namely: (1) an airplane was used incapable of flying on the disability of one engine, and (2) there were inadequate landing facilities. I think it is fair to assume that in this particular case if either one of these two principles had not been violated there would have been no injury to the personnel of the plane.

A Remarkable Record

In the United States the whole short history of regular passenger services over organized airways using multi-engined planes indicates a total mileage of 2,200,000, carrying 44,650 passengers up to June 27, 1929. There has been but a single accident resulting in death or injury. This accident, in which three passengers were killed, was a most abnormal one caused by the pilot of another plane actually "stunting" into the passenger plane in utter disregard of flying regulations and with no respect for human life.

Because this type of flying is in its infancy in the United States, uninformed popular opinion is under the impression that we still trail Europe in commercial aviation. Nothing could be further from the truth. There are today approximately 3,000 commercial and civil airplanes in operation in all of the countries of the world, excluding the United States, and there are 71 aircraft factories in these countries. On the other hand, in the United States there are to-day approximately 7,100 commercial and civil airplanes in operation and about 180 airplane factories of record, of which about 55 are on a production basis.

The second kind of flying with which we are concerned is the personal use of an airplane in much the same way as one uses an automobile. The hindrance to the universal use of airplanes in this way today is certain aerodynamic features of aircraft which impose the need of far too much skill and experience on the part of the pilot.

In order to hasten this day of universal flying, the Daniel Guggenheim Fund for the Promotion of Aeronautics two years ago organized a Safe Aircraft Competition, which will take place this summer.* The interest manifested both here and abroad promises that the results will be of very great importance in developing an aerodynamically safe plane. For the development of private flying, which may eventually reach the extent of private automobile travel, we are now seeking through this competition to make the airplane not merely a machine that is safe in very skilled hands, but one that is fool-proof under all kinds of conditions and can be safely operated by an ordinary lay-pilot.

The Plane of Tomorrow

We want, in short, a plane that will be able to land more slowly, take off more quickly and climb more steeply, make

---

*June, 1929.

both flatter and steeper glides, and which will remain under control at all speeds and altitudes, even when the pilot, owing to weather conditions, is unable to maintain an even keel. The fundamentally unsafe aerodynamic feature in the airplane of the past has been the inability to maintain controls at low speeds. Two revolutionary developments have recently taken place pointing the way to overcome this difficulty.

The first is the so-called "slot" which I shall attempt to explain very briefly, invented by an Englishman, Mr. Handley Page. An airplane is sustained in the air due to an even flow of air rushing not only under, but far more important, above, its wings. In the past, if the normal airplane were permitted to reduce its speed to below, say, fifty miles per hour, it became necessary to fly at such an angle that the air flow over the wings became uneven, which resulted in loss of control. Mr. Handley Page has invented a simple automatic device, "the slot," which is a small auxiliary wing placed at the forward edge of the main wing and prevents the uneven flow of the air and hence loss of control at low speeds.

The second is the autogiro invented by a Spaniard, Mr. De la Cierva. The autogiro is unlike the normal airplane in that instead of the usual fixed wings it has wings that revolve freely around a shaft coming up from the body of the airplane. In this aircraft the wings move quickly even though the plane itself is moving slowly, and hence sustention is maintained and there is no loss of control at the lowest speeds. In case of engine failure in the autogiro the wings continue revolving like a windmill, allowing the aircraft to descend in the manner of a parachute on a

steep slow glide to earth.   Both of these inventions will be submitted for the competition.

The supervision of this project is one of the particular duties
of Captain Emory S. Land (CC), U. S. N.   Through the courtesy of the Navy Department, Captain Land, who is one of the
ablest of the officers of the Navy, has received a leave of absence
to help us in our attempts at the solution of some of the fundamental problems in aviation.

THE FOG HAZARD

We are confronted with one unsolved primary problem in
flying and that is ability to fly and land safely in fog.   This
problem is really one of punctuality of air travel rather than
safety; for the experienced pilot follows the rule that Colonel
Lindbergh invariably uses, namely, "Do not attempt to fly
through fog but turn back and land before it is too late."

In an effort to establish this problem we have established
a full flight laboratory where we are testing and developing
the various means of overcoming this hindrance to air traffic.
In the preliminary stages of some of our test flights, one of the
two pilots at the dual controls will be enclosed by a hood so that
he cannot see outside the plane and must fly exclusively by
instruments.   This will simulate the condition of flying through
fog, without its dangers.   The chief operator of our laboratory is Lieut. James H. Doolittle, assigned through the courtesy
of the Army Air Corps.   He combines the rare qualities of
the highly trained scientist with those of one of the most experienced and accomplished pilots in the world.   His technical

assistant is Professor William G. Brown of Massachusetts Institute of Technology. In co-operation with important agencies in this country and abroad, we hope before long to demonstrate that it is feasible to fly safely and land safely on a prepared airport through fog.

GENERAL SAFETY PRECAUTIONS

There is no reason why today the public should not fly with confidence, but before doing so they should make sure that there exists the following in the passenger air transport system that they would patronize:

1. Multi-engine planes capable of flying on the disability of at least one engine.
2. Two pilots licensed by the Government.
3. Planes and engines licensed by the Government.
4. Adequate landing facilities over the route to be flown.
5. Intensive weather reporting service over the route to be flown.
6. Wireless or at least a visual communication system between the plane and the airway.
7. Last, and most important of all, responsibility of the operators of the air service.

Rest assured that today flying is on the threshold of acceptance by the individuals of the civilized world for their own use. The almost limitless unobstructed air above the tree tops, without intersecting highways swarming with traffic, offers the safest travel lanes. It remains for man to take advantage of them.

EUROPEAN FLYING IMPRESSIONS

Based on a 3,600-Mile Air Tour Recently Completed

BY DANIEL ROCHFORD
Aviation Editor, Boston Herald

IF you've walked around inside the wing of a monster airplane without having to stoop; if you've watched them building passenger waiting rooms and recreation promenades as big as half the Harvard Stadium bent straight; if you've talked to the pilots of a big tri-motor at London one day and found the same fellows clear out on the Russian frontier a few days later and clocked them into Vienna and Paris and realized that they fly every big route in Europe and that their comrades are doing the same trick; if you know European Diesel engines have flown successfully all winter; if you've toured airplane factories where there is one engineer for every ten workmen; if you've visited flying schools where boys have to pay only twenty-five dollars per month for their food, lodging, and flying instruction; if you've talked to sightseeing pilots who have been flying in single-motored airplanes out around the spit of the Jungfrau, Mont Blanc and down the canyons of the Alps for eight years with never a passenger casualty; if you've done some of these things, you're not going to come home from Europe and say that America has bought everything Europe has in aviation.

Going over on the boat in March, an Austrian war ace, now engineer at Junkers, said to me, "In America you have wonderful enthusiasm and tremendous aerial activity. But in design you are as little children." We pooh-poohed him. A month later he showed us the new Junkers forty-passenger plane in the factory at Dessau. There was a fuselage as big as a railroad car. We climbed up into the wings, walked into them. We looked at the water-cooled engines, mounted inside the wings, huge thousand-horsepower creatures which will drive air screws on shafts out in front of the wings. Over each motor, electric lights. Cut out one engine completely, overhaul it in flight, flying on the others. No air stream bothering the mechanic. Cool the same motor with this new lighter-than-water fluid. Air-cooled engines, he said, are no good in the power ranges above five hundred horses. Junkers has abandoned attempts to use them. With the protected engine inside the wing, air-cooling is out of the question anyway. We looked around the vast cabin which extends right into the wings. We apologized to him for disputing him on the steamer.

When you stop to realize the number of great new planes they are completing in Europe and the paucity of such pioneering construction in America, it makes you wonder. France has an airplane with wings you can walk through. The Handley-Page people in England have a new biplane with the passenger cabin below the bottom wing and with four engines, two between and two above. Dornier's new 12-engined flying boat is designed to carry 100 passengers on transatlantic service.

In Paris we climbed into a new Blériot mock-up of a twin passenger-compartmented monoplane with engines above the wing and passengers below. We admired the great four-engined Rohrbachs at Travemundi.

At Dessau we talked with Chief Pilot Zimmerman and Pilot Risticz, world endurance record holders. "Are you not nervous about your first flight in the big Junkers?"

"No. We know what it will do. I have six other pilots here. All wish to make the first flight. All are capable." I mentioned how much I'd like to return to Germany to see it fly. "Oh, stay where you are," he answered, smiling. "We'll bring it over to you."

Faced by evidences of tremendous aviation development throughout Europe, one realizes, nevertheless, that America is sweeping along at a pace which is rapidly absorbing the best that Europe has to offer.

Go down and land on any big European airport and go into the hangars for private and sport planes. You find a surprisingly small number of little planes. Of course, private pilots are discouraged by a healthy landing fee from using such fields as Croydon. But on the other hand, such chief airports as Switzerland's Dubendorf, principal military and commercial center, encourage private machines. The canton even maintains a hangar there and grants free storage. Down at Lyon, in southern France, we saw old early-war vintage equipment being flown privately, equipment which our inspectors would ground without a second glance. Cities of 300,000 population have three or four privately owned planes.

It's a money question. Young fellows who can't afford to own automobiles are certainly not going to be sporting airplanes. If it weren't for the flying clubs which are supported by the communities and give flying at no cost at all or a nominal charge, the boys of several countries over there would not pilot power planes at all. The German glider schools charge the amazingly small sum of twenty-five dollars for the month including everything. Yet that sum is a tremendous obstacle to most young Germans. Even in England where private flying clubs have done best, they howl against the dropping of the subsidies, and many fliers oppose this new association of flying clubs which hopes to link England in an airport net, because it has a new form of subsidy the existing clubs have not.

There is where America has the advantage. Perhaps we are a bit too cocky about what our money can buy. But enough of it seems to be able to accomplish anything. We flew around Europe in the propeller wash of Clarence Young, so to speak. He rode his own plane, while we flew 3,600 miles on the various airlines. But his speeches had stirred them all up. Almost every pilot or radio man we talked with managed to get in a few questions about pay and promotion in the States. Over there a pilot is paid about $135 a month and five cents per mile and knows he is lucky. Here we even tell the newspapers that we have to pay our pilots $6,000 a year to ride around in tri-motors.

Too many Americans judge European airlines by one ride from Paris to London. Or they see Tempelhof and come home and tell their friends that American airports don't know how to handle planes or weather services.

Naturally, you can't go to Europe in the spring during the bad weather and come home and expect your generalities to be without serious discrepancies. But nobody can put in forty hours in many types of planes and through various countries, and not see a few things worth reporting.

The American likes to have a cut-and-dried yes or no to his question. Is American passenger carrying as good as European or not? In point of service offered to the man who wants to go places by airplane, it is not as good as central Europe's, because we have not the many feeder lines on scheduled service. And further, it won't be as good, because, unless we adopt a government subsidy, we can't have the many short schedule flights they have in Europe.

Remember that the Luft Hansa, the greatest air system in Europe, earns about one-fifth of its operating costs. Realize that the British, with an ideal run between London and Paris, were not able to earn more than about two-thirds of their expenses last year. Even the Swiss, who do charter flying out around the Alps, earn only three-quarters of their costs.

They don't beat about the bush over there when you talk costs. They admit that the feeder lines do not pay and never will. The Luft Hansa, for example, has three forms of subsidy. The central government pays on mileage of planes flying from a point inside Germany to a point outside. The provinces which correspond to our states do similarly. The small cities and towns, which have perhaps one plane a day each way, split the mileage cost between them.

It may be argued that feeder lines will ultimately develop real traffic in America. Let us hope so. But they haven't done it in Europe. And even the main lines, with fares clear down where they touch whiskers with railroad fares, fly the run with almost empty ships days on days during the winter season. My wife and I had several rides as the sole occupants of ten and twelve passenger planes. Too many Americans see European flying only in the summer when business is best and weather most favorable.

In point of air travel over what lines we have, America is just as good as, and in several ways, better than, Europe. We're faster for one thing. I've flown many round trips between New York and Boston on Colonial Tri-motored Wasp Fords. They give you 125 miles an hour against Europe's 95. Bus facilities at terminals are excellent. A steward serves you sandwiches and ginger ale en route, provided he hasn't forgotten one or both. You couldn't ask for a more comfortable ride.

But Colonial doesn't weight its loads, yet. It's going to when some new hangars are built, but it doesn't today. Its ships don't have straps in the seats. They don't have a light at the front of the plane which flashes on as the plane is about to land and warns, "Fasten your seat straps; landing!"

On the other hand, Americans who had flown abroad had told me about the perfect weather system. And I sat in a single-motored plane whose pilot was fighting a blinding snowstorm for thirty minutes to get down, finally between the four towering smokestacks which make Dresden's airport such a comfort once you're on it. The weather system left us right where it leaves so many other airplanes, at the toss of your pilot's ability. If he knows his stuff, you get down the way you want to. If he doesn't, you get down the other way.

One thing that shocked me was the absence of wheel brakes on the European airliners. Why, we were never able to learn. Some of the newer ships are coming out with them.

Nor are the European inspection systems superhuman. We had a good wait after starting time at Copenhagen while they pulled some bad plugs. The human factor remains the same, no matter what sort of inspection systems you install.

We mentioned Paris to London. A ride over that route would be better in monoplanes. Those multi-motored biplanes cut off your visibility below and give you all the noise. The high-wing monoplane is best for passenger visibility, but the engine noises are thrown down into the cabin. The low-wing monoplane is better for eliminating noise, but not quite as good for visibility.

Frankly, that low-winged Junkers impressed me more than anything else in Europe. I clocked the Junkers single-motor and tri-motor in flight, load for load, against such high-wing monoplanes as the Dornier-Merker, Fokker and Foeke-Wulf. The low-wing, because of the rolling cushion of air close to the ground, took off every time from five to twelve seconds more quickly, requiring from seven to thirteen seconds, as against from eleven to twenty-two seconds, load for load.

The low-wing as developed by Junkers should be carefully studied in America.   If, as it seems, it can get off more quickly and slows up much faster as it approaches the ground to land, those are tremendously important recommendations.   And it has a wonderful safety argument in the fact that the big metal wing is beneath the cabin and in ninety-nine out of a hundred crashes the wing would wash out first, sparing the cabin.

Speaking of airplane noise, there is food for thought in what Maxim found out up at Hartford a little while ago.   He has developed some new airplane engine mufflers.   He sent a sound engineer up with Harry Copland, and they muffled the engine noises almost completely.   They found that the strict engine noises are only about one-fifth the total airplane noise.   And they found, too, that most airplane noise comes in through the floor of the plane.

Our weather and radio reporting service is fast reaching satisfactory growth.   Europeans have been using radio on their bigger planes and have the thing down so well that, during a flight over from Holland to Hamburg, we climbed up above two cloud levels and at 8,000 feet got a radio check of our exact location within a few minutes of our inquiry.   Flying into Danzig one afternoon through localized snowstorms, we were told by radio to go beyond the south of the city and then swing back in from the sea behind snow.   We did and got in nicely. At Croydon they showed us how they can bring a plane right in over the field in fog.   But the sets in the planes weren't held out to us for personal radio telephone conversations with towns on the course.

The Europeans have done a good stunt for passenger insurance. The various lines are formed into an international union. Seven per cent of every fare collected is paid into an insurance fund, and from this stated sums are paid for injuries or casualties. The Germans made this insurance compulsory. The French offered it, but did not require it. The Swiss, English, Austrians, Dutch, Scandinavians, and Russians followed the Luft Hansa lead.

Terminal airports, as might be imagined where governments aid with such subsidies, are large and excellent in Europe. I had never dreamed of such huge buildings as those of the enlarged Hamburg airport, for example. You could build a second story inside the great hangars and double their capacity. The waiting room and offices tower five stories and stretch across the whole side of the field. The fields themselves are turfed and have wide paved or hard surfaced areas joining hangars and, in some cases, even extending out as runways into the field. Dessau has a 3,000-foot paved take-off strip with a mile or so flat field beyond it. There they will launch the new super-Junkers. Danzig has two strips on different sides of the field.

The motor starting was also interesting. Compressed air in cylinders is wheeled out and a speedy hose connection made and "presto" she roars.

A conspicuous feature of German airports was the police with flags standing out on the field. They have a great number of men standing around doing jobs which other airports leave undone. Practically all airports in Europe use a man in the observation tower to flag planes on to and off the fields. Sirens are sounded as planes come in to warn craft on the ground. And planes taking off must get the "all clear" signal from the tower. But the Germans also have men on the field where you turn your plane for the take-off, and they flag you away like an auto race official.

The Germans are very honest about their Luft Hansa. They admit candidly that "we have no military aviation so we must develop the Luft Hansa." That explains why the pilots are sent around the circuit to learn all European airways. That explains the generosity with numbers of employees on the fields. That accounts for much of the development in factories. We were in Germany during the reparations conference in Paris. While we were there, the Germans lopped thirty million marks from the army budget, and vast sums from the Luft Hansa. They were just playing good poker. It would be pretty hard to plead poverty and be spending large sums on maneuvers and airline extensions.

But the people do not scheme war. They hope that their peace-time airplanes can prove of some defense in case their security is questioned. It is my conviction, and I had a chance to get to know many Germans, including former soldiers and officers, that Germany is fed up on war. But I did hear such talk as that France, being allied to Jugo-Slavia which was at swords' points with Italy, might find herself suddenly at war with Italy via Germany. And the Germans fear a war fought on German soil.

Several European airports used flocks of sheep as lawn mowers. And most of them have fences to keep the general public off

and out. One of the best things I saw, which can be used
everywhere in this country at no great expense, was the use
of smoke on the flying fields for wind indicators. They have
smoke cones which burn a chemical giving off white smoke.
Or they use a common smoke candle. You can refill the holders and stick a new one in the ground as the old one burns
out. When one realizes how many American fields have spent
good money for these rigid wooden or metal wind indicators
which always point in some direction, even when there isn't
any wind at all, it seems too bad. Even a wind sock, which,
if it is soft enough, can hang limp or stretch taut with the wind
conditions, is inferior to smoke. Smoke trails out across the
field and shows you velocity as well as direction and local surface
vagaries of the wind. If a smoke candle is burned in the center of a circle in the runways, no pilot can miss it or need waste
time trying to find the wind cone on a hangar some place.

European night flying of passengers is limited still to the
Luft Hansa Berlin-Hanover and Berlin-Königsberg runs. Berths
have been built into some planes, but undressing and getting
into an airplane bed is still an event of the ordinary air traveler's future. In the winter season and until May, the night
runs were not operated. Similarly the great flying boat runs
up to Copenhagen and the Scandinavias were not possible
because of the ice in the Baltic and North seas. And the
Russian services were shut down until spring rains and melted
snows were gone from the flying fields in May. The trans-Alps
services of the British and French likewise bow to the winter
season.

The European pilot is the same sort of fellow who flies over here. He is a wonderful, generous, capable chap. No matter what language he speaks you can sputter along in air language and understand him. He is interested in what we are doing in America. But he is not jealous, and he's glad to talk and show you what they've got in Europe.

PRESENT STATUS OF COMMERCIAL AERONAUTICS IN EUROPE

BY HON. CLARENCE M. YOUNG

Assistant Secretary of Commerce for Aeronautics

PRACTICALLY every important capital in Europe is now served by one or more airlines. Austria, Belgium, Czecho-Slovakia, Denmark, Finland, France, Germany, Great Britain, Hungary, Italy, the Netherlands, Poland, Russia, Spain, Sweden, Switzerland, all are utilizing aircraft. Despite the handicap of numerous near-by international borders, air commerce in Europe has grown steadily.

Last year, German planes, for example, flew 7,030,565 miles, carried 115,000 passengers, handled 1,130,000 pounds of mail, and transported 4,282,000 pounds of baggage and express. France was not far behind with 3,753,133 miles flown in regular service, 21,000 passengers carried, 1,607,280 pounds of mail and 2,755,000 pounds of baggage and express. Although the figures for other European nations might also be cited, suffice it to say that practically every country in Europe is making large strides in civil aeronautics.

Last year, for example, the postal administration of Spain started a service whereby mail for international air transport is received by Spanish post offices for sixteen different European nations.   The Italian government is encouraging the use of private aircraft, both of national and of foreign registration, by providing airport facilities and services.   During the first three months of operation of the through lines, more than five tons of mail were carried between England and India.   Great Britain has, in addition to its numerous scheduled airlines, thirteen subsidized flying clubs and five independent ones.   These subsidized flying clubs at the end of 1928 had 3,288 members, as compared with only 780 three years earlier, and now have 420 qualified pilots.

As an instance of the services available in Europe, air mail from Berlin is delivered in London by noon of the following day.   On the return flight, mail leaving London at 8:15 in the morning arrives at Berlin at 5:25 the same afternoon.   A combination of train-plane service permits the transfer of mail between Berlin and Barcelona, Spain, in twenty-four hours.

As an example of the rapid developments taking place in European air commerce, consider the history of a single company in Germany, the Deutsche Luft Hansa, which started operating thirty airlines in April, 1926, and added twenty-four additional lines within a few months.   This number had increased to ninety by the summer of 1928; of these, eighty-four were operated by the company and six were maintained in co-operation with foreign countries.   Special express services are now operated between London, Amsterdam, Hanover, and Berlin, and between Paris, Cologne, Easen, Mulheim, and Berlin.   As the result of an agreement entered into between this company and the German Imperial Railways, express can now be sent to any place in Germany where there is a railway station, through the combined utilization of air and rail transport. Following the successful introduction of the through air and rail service in 1927, the Luft Hansa arranged with the German railroad company for the transfer of passengers, effective September 1, 1928. Passengers may start a journey by air or first-class railway and change to the other at will, and with but little formality.

The Imperial Airways, Limited, of London, maintains a regular passenger, mail and express service between London and Paris—a distance of 225 miles—making one to five round trips per day. During the eight years ended March 1, 1929, Great Britain's government spent approximately $19,000,000 for the promotion of civil air transportation. In Germany, too, the national and local governments aid generously in the promotion of air transportation—spending some $20,000,000 annually for this purpose. France's 1929 appropriation for aeronautics amounted to over $70,000,000.

Because of the steady growth of air transportation in Europe, there have been developed a number of excellent airports. Three of these airports are outstanding: Croydon at London, Le Bourget at Paris, and Tempelhof at Berlin. Each is approximately 400 acres in area, has similar ground equipment, accommodates similar traffic, and exercises about the same type of control over activities. Moreover, the respective governments of all three adhere to the International Convention of 1919 which makes them all amenable to practically uniform regulations.

There is a sufficient difference in the local management, however, to warrant separate reference to each.

CROYDON AIRDROME (LONDON)

The Croydon Airdrome, which is frequently referred to as the London Terminal Aerodrome, is located near the village of Croydon on the outskirts of London; it is within about one mile of a suburban train station, and can be reached by bus, automobile or taxicab. Since it takes from forty-five minutes to an hour to reach it from downtown London, depending upon street traffic and train service, this time element is not favorable, especially when considered in connection with the comparatively short flights of about two and a half hours to Paris and Brussels. Apparently the determining factor in the selection of this site was available area.

The administration building at Croydon is extremely well arranged. On the first floor is a large, well-equipped waiting room with the ticket and information offices of the various airlines opening into it on all sides through a series of alcoves. There are also provided a buffet, news stand, ladies' waiting room, and a large map of the various air routes showing weather conditions at various locations. This map is kept current, and a very interesting method of showing departures and arrivals of airplanes is maintained.

An enclosed passage, in which passport and other formalities are observed, leads from the waiting room to the airdrome. This corridor, which is part of the building, terminates at the platform upon which the departing plane is awaiting its passengers. When passengers board the plane, their luggage has already been placed aboard by attendants and properly stowed away. Another passage leading from the airdrome to the waiting room is quite similar except that it takes the passengers through the customs office, as well as through the passport corridor.

Here again the luggage causes the passenger no annoyance; it is taken from the plane to the customs counter for examination in his presence, and from there to the airline's bus or to the passenger's other means of transportation. There are no other entrances or exits either to or from the airdrome. There are, however, suitable places where motor cars may be parked and where the public may sit or stand to watch activities, but they are outside the enclosure of the airdrome landing field.

The second floor of the administration building contains a large number of office rooms which are occupied by the airdrome staff, including the weather bureau, the aircraft inspectors, and airdrome officers. Other offices on this floor are leased to various airlines for the use of clerical personnel and local representatives; and still others are available for expansion as activities increase.

An integral part of the administration building is a four-story tower at the side of the airdrome, which is surmounted by a radio mast. This tower contains a chart or map room and a radio room; from a platform surrounding it, traffic signals are displayed controlling the movements of arriving and departing planes.

Immediately adjoining the administration building is a freight and merchandise building for storage and customs purposes. A short distance away is a privately operated hotel, which has comfortable rooms, ample restaurant facilities, and a roof which has been made available for guests wishing to observe airdrome activities.

The hangars and shops are of conventional type and are located in the vicinity of the administration building—the shops for engine repair, overhaul and testing, being in the rear of the hangar line.   All buildings are, of course, of fireproof construction.

Among the several different airlines operating from the Croydon Airdrome are Luft Hansa (Germany), Imperial Airways (Great Britain), Air Union (France), Sabena (Belgium), and Royal Dutch or K. L. M. (Holland).   Each line maintains fixed schedules; and arrivals and departures are a matter of regularity which naturally contributes materially to the control of activities. Each plane, upon arriving, whether in scheduled operation or otherwise, must taxi to the platform, or "tarmac" as it is called, and report in; and the same is true of departing planes, which must taxi from the platform to the point of take-off and there receive a signal from the tower before starting the take-off run.

Only a relatively small amount of itinerant or non-scheduled flying is done at this airport.   Flying instruction for the most part is carried on at flying clubs located elsewhere.   This means that the dominating activity at Croydon is scheduled service.

LE BOURGET AIRPORT (PARIS)

The most famous airport in France is Le Bourget, located on the outskirts of Paris at about the same distance from downtown

Paris as is Croydon from London. There is a street car service most of the way; but inasmuch as this is somewhat devious and comparatively slow, the best way to reach the airport is by automobile, bus or taxicab. Under normal traffic conditions the airport can be reached in about forty-five minutes.

Like Croydon, Le Bourget comprises approximately 400 acres, and the arrangement of buildings with respect to the landing area is quite similar. The administration building, however, is not as elaborate, nor does it contain as great a variety of activities—the meteorological and radio stations being located in a smaller building near by. Entrance to the airdrome is effected through a customs and passport room, above which is an excellent restaurant. There is an observation tower on which an airdrome employee is constantly stationed for the purpose of observing aircraft operations both on the airdrome and in the air. The hangars are located on either side of the main building.

The flying field proper is, of course, suitably enclosed, and no one is admitted except the airdrome staff, airline employees, passengers entering through the customs office, and other persons having business therein. Adequate parking and observation area is provided outside the enclosure. In addition to the several organizations already enumerated, which use Croydon as a terminus, there are two or three other French lines operating from Le Bourget. There are also rather important local operations, taking passengers on sightseeing trips over Paris and environs.

As at Croydon, each arriving aircraft must proceed to the platform in front of the customs office and report in. Departing aircraft must also leave from the same place before taxying to the point of take-off.

Tempelhof Airport (Berlin)

Germany's chief airport, Tempelhof Airdrome, is located within the city limits of Berlin, approximately fifteen minutes from the business section by automobile or bus. It now serves twenty-nine different airlines. Street cars pass within a comparatively short walking distance, and the service is sufficiently frequent for convenient use. Indicative of the ease with which this airdrome is reached, it is not uncommon for 20,000 people to visit it during a summer week-end when aircraft activities are at their height. Ample facilities for comfort and entertainment are provided, and the airdrome takes on a gala atmosphere upon the slightest provocation, even though a small admission charge is ordinarily made. The proximity of the airdrome to the city is a decided advantage and makes it extremely popular, not only with the interested observers, but with the users of air transport as well. On one occasion recently, more than 200,000 visitors assembled there to pay respects to some returning aviator of note.

The buildings, including administration, hangars, and shops, are arranged in conventional manner along one side of the airdrome, the center of the group being the administration building. This building contains the offices of the various airport companies, as well as the radio and weather rooms, post office, customs office, airport restaurant, waiting room, and the traffic offices of Deutsche Luft Hansa.

As is the case at Croydon, entrance to the airdrome is effected through the customs and passport offices by way of a canopied corridor to the loading platform. Immediately in front of the administration building and on either side of the entrance corridor is a large enclosure provided with tables and chairs, which constitutes an outdoor restaurant and beer garden. Between it and the loading platform is yet another enclosure to which spectators are admitted.

In front of the administration building is a control tower from which all aircraft traffic, whether incoming or outgoing, is controlled by signals from the airdrome police. Five permanent hangars, of fireproof construction and unusual size, are located on either side of the administration building; they are provided with steel doors electrically driven and opening horizontally. Between the hangars are large repair shops, well equipped with overhead carriers, supplies, tools and machinery. Between two of the hangars is located an underground fuel tank of 40,000 litres capacity; in front of another is a 20,000-litre tank; and in front of a third is a 100,000-litre tank, the latter being equipped with electrically driven, centrally controlled pumps.

The entire airdrome is surrounded by a substantial fence, and in addition to obstruction lights, beacons, etc., the effective landing area is enclosed with boundary markers made up of neon tube units about seven feet in length spaced at approximately 300-foot intervals. An unusual but very desirable feature of this port's equipment is a broad, hard-surfaced apron extending the entire length of the hangar line. Approximately 300 feet in width, this apron greatly facilitates the maneuvering of planes in and out of the hangars and taxying to and from the loading station in front of the administration building.

A hotel has not yet been provided, but it is believed existing plans contemplate the enlargement of the administration building or the addition of a suitable building for that purpose. Meanwhile the restaurant concession has been let to the Mitrops, an organization which operates the dining cars on the railroads in Germany and which also has the buffet privileges on the Luft Hansa airliners.

My recent survey of European airports convinced me that three things are fundamentally applicable to airport management and administration in the United States: (1) Adequate jurisdiction with a qualified executive in charge; (2) definite control of all activities, including their segregation when possible and advisable; and (3) uniform rules and regulations governing the operation of aircraft in the vicinity of the airport, and in landing and taking off.   I am also convinced that the problem of airport management can be successfully handled without difficulty, if a competent executive with suitable authority exercises intelligent control over all activities, in conformity with uniform requirements.

A combination of reliability, comfort, and speed is fundamental to the successful operation of any air transport system, whether it be in the United States, Europe, or elsewhere.   This involves practically all elements entering into such a system— aircraft, pilots, ground personnel and equipment, airways, schedule maintenance, radio and weather service, and adequate airports.   Fortunately, services operating wholly within the

United States are not concerned with the more or less annoying business of passports and customs caused by the many border crossings in Europe. Many of the air journeys there, even though they are of only two or three hours' duration, place one in several different countries, with different languages, different customs and the usual examination of passports and luggage, formalities and immigration, public health, etc. Here, we can fly almost 3,000 miles and still be in the same country. Consequently, we seldom, if ever, see or hear of a passport or customs official, unless, of course, one of the several existing international services is used. This is a distinct advantage, and will react most favorably on our air transport system.

Despite this important advantage, however, American manufacturers and operators realize that they can profit by the long operating experience of the European lines, and numbers of representatives of our aeronautic industry have visited Europe at various times for the purpose of studying their methods. One thing which they have learned from Europe is the importance of details, the refinement of comparatively minor things which either irritate or gratify the users of air transport. The manner in which passengers are transported to and from the airport, the facility with which their luggage is handled for them, the ease with which they are transferred to and from the aircraft, their comfort in the plane while enroute, all furnish examples of these details and refinements.

Although the actual transportation from one airport to another may seem to dominate all other phases, the passenger will not overlook the fact that he was obliged to trundle his own luggage in a taxi to the airport, to find his own way to the aircraft by way of the propeller blast, or to locate his own seat reservation.   Nor does he like to amuse himself en route by wondering over what location he is passing, by asking himself whether the aircraft is on schedule, or wondering where a blanket can be found when altitude makes the cabin chilly, or why the belt contraption is placed on his seat, or why the aircraft bounces around in rough air without knowing that it is a normal condition in particular localities.   American air transport lines have already recognized the importance of these and numerous other similar details, and are giving very careful consideration to the comfort and convenience of the traveling public.   Most European lines, too, have given this phase of air transport a great deal of thought, and that is one reason why these lines have been so highly regarded.

Because of America's freedom from international boundaries, great distances between centers of population, high standards of living, density of commerce and other inherent advantages, the development of a great air transport system is inevitable.   Already American airplanes are flying more than 80,000 miles per day; already we have more than 15,000 miles of fully equipped airways; already we have a thousand airports, both municipal and commercial, in active operation, with an additional 1,200 either proposed or in the process of construction; and a number of the former are rapidly becoming the equal of any of the famous airports of the world.

It is necessary to be mindful that practically all of this has been accomplished within a period of three years, without direct government subsidy, and by private enterprise entirely. During that brief period of time, the air transport organizations have been able to train personnel and gain valuable operating experience, the aircraft manufacturer has concentrated on the design of aircraft especially adapted to transportation needs, and the Department of Commerce has made substantial progress in the development and establishment of a comprehensive airways system fully equipped with all known aids to air navigation. It all provides a most advantageous promise for the further extension of the air transportation services of the United States, whether for mail, merchandise or passengers, to any extent for which there can possibly be a demand.

NOTE—Paper presented at the American Roadbuilders' Convention at Washington, D.C., October 25, 1929.

THE MONSTER DORNIER DO.X

A German Experiment in Gigantic Air Cruisers

BY JOHN H. D. BLANKE

THERE has been much discussion in the last few years as to the practicability of heavier-than-air planes capable of large scale transoceanic transport. The factors of safety and economy in a service of this type make huge construction practically a necessity.

Engineers and builders have generally viewed the practical possibility with negative eyes. The recent trial flight of the three-decked all-steel Do.X at Lake Constance, Switzerland, has consequently held the undivided attention of manufacturers, engineers and operators throughout the world.

Much speculation in reference to the lift and handling possibilities of the huge craft was erased when it took off easily at its first launching, rising into the air after a run of only five hundred yards. At a subsequent trial powered by its twelve Siemens-Jupiter motors, with a combined efficiency of 6300 h.p., it rose to a ceiling of 6500 feet with a full load. The great ship seemed to handle with the greatest ease and its builder, Dr. Claudius Dornier, expressed the idea that it came fully up to all expectations of performance.

135

Contrary to conclusions of other builders, it is Dr. Dornier's belief that the larger the construction, the greater the efficiency. He intends to demonstrate the correctness of this point by the use of the Do.X for transatlantic and long haul commercial flying.

The Do.X is a monoplane with high set wings of the cantilever type, with a span of 157.4 feet.

The wings fastened laterally to the top of the hull are additionally joined by three struts to the combined stub wings and floats projecting from the lower part of the hull. This peculiarity of design is reputed to give great lateral stability to the ship, and to help reduce take-off run for a quick lift. In the air they give additional lifting surface. The total bearing surface is 5300 square feet. The wings' interiors provide a gangway sufficiently large for motor inspection and repair.

The motors are of nine cylinder, radial air-cooled type, each developing 500 to 525 h.p., and are mounted in line back to back. They are supported by a stream-lined structure opening up into the gangway inside the wings, thus making them completely accessible during flight. Each motor operates as an individual unit and may be shut down independently. All motors respond to single electrical control.

The r.p.m. of each motor is indicated individually, and a complete set of gauges in both pilot's and engineer's room enables immediate and accurate check-up of all units at all times.

The ship has tremendous reserve power, and it is stated that four, or even five, may drop out of action without the ship losing altitude. The accessibility previously mentioned provides for the possibilities of repair in the event of motor failure, and in consequence insures against forced landings due to engines falling into trouble or going dead. It is further claimed that the capability of the power plant is so great that the motors may be throttled forty per cent immediately after the take-off.

The hull is built on the general lines of a glider. The bows are of rather V-shaped section flat at the bottom. This ends in a step at about four-tenths of the hull's 131.4 feet over all. From the step a short keel starts, and ends further down in a small rudder for navigation, behind which the boat's bottom has a very flat V-form tapering towards the tail.

Inside the hull there are three decks, each with ample head room, and subdivided by several water-tight bulkheads. The lowest deck holds the fuel tanks, loose equipment, stores, goods, etc.

The middle deck is the main one and is reserved entirely for passengers. It is 66 feet long without kitchen, and dependent on the desires of the transport company, may be provided with rooms for day accommodation, special entertainment rooms, or sleeping rooms. It, of course, may be appointed in any fashion to meet the demands of the public it services. For use in long distance flights, the rear section of the fuselage may also be separated from the passenger cabins by a special partition so that it may serve as accommodation for a substitute crew shift.

The third deck is built on the order of a large cabin. The forward end, fitted with large, all-vision windows, forms the pilot's compartment. Directly back of it is the navigation room, which also serves for the commander and his first mate. Then follows the engineer's room. He, with four mechanics, is responsible for the technical detail of the boat and its motors. From this room start the gangways leading right and left into the wings and the motors above them. These gangways also hold the gasoline and oil lines, which may be kept constantly under observation. In the engineer's room is also a complete set of gauges for the control of all motors. It also contains an auxiliary motor which drives a dynamo to supply current for lighting the ship and for running the many indicators and other instruments.

The last compartment of the third deck holds the wireless room.

No wood is used in the ship, the entire construction being of steel and duralumin.

The cruising speed is 120 m.p.h. Her maximum speed is calculated at 150 m.p.h.

The twelve motors were designed to lift a load of fifty tons, but it is now believed will permit a take-off with better than sixty tons.

The published estimates of carrying capacity of one hundred passengers and crew, are, of course, dependent on the length of flight and consequent weight of gasoline load. For long hauls a pay load of ten tons is estimated. For short distances this may be increased to as much as twenty-five tons (exhaustive tests have not yet indicated these as complete figures and they are consequently largely surmise).

The Do.X maneuvers easily under single pilot handling, although dual control is provided.

It is claimed for the ship that the relative location of motor room and fuel tanks, and the ready and free accessibility of fuel lines, is such as to make the danger of fire very remote. As an added precaution against explosion, protective gas is utilizable in the fuel rooms.

As a matter of some importance it is to be noted that the big boat operated with exceptional quietness in the test flights.

CANADA HONORS THE FIRST ATLANTIC FLYERS

BY GUY E. RHOADES

OFFICIAL honor and commemoration of the names of Sir John Alcock and Sir Arthur Whitten Brown was given by the Dominion government on July, 1929, when Brigadier General A. H. Bell, officer commanding Military District No. 2, christened two Royal Canadian Air Force "Siskin" pursuit planes, naming them after the two intrepid fliers, first conquerors of the Atlantic.

It was just a little over ten years ago that Captain Jack Alcock and Lieutenant Arthur Whitten Brown took off from St. John, Newfoundland, bound on the greatest adventure in aviation up to that time. They left at 5:15 in the afternoon, and at 9:40 the next morning landed at Clifton, Ireland. They had flown approximately 1,900 miles in the remarkable time of a little over sixteen hours.

Since that time flights across the Atlantic from west to east have been accomplished by a number of aviators who have possessed better machines and better engines, the result of experience gained during the course of time in engineering.

Recent Atlantic flights performed in cabin planes with powerful engines and with every possible aid to navigation look pale beside the feat of these two men who flew their Vickers "Vimy" biplane, powered with two Rolls-Royce engines, drove it through rain, sleet, snow and fog on to a glorious finish, 1,900 miles across water.

Alcock and Brown were favored by a following wind, but they were not favored by the weather apart from that. Occasionally they would catch their breath as they emerged from a dense bank of fog to find that they were on the verge of flying into the sea. All night they flew in the wet and cold, half blinded by the rain and sleet which beat in their faces, or unable to see through the fog which lay opaque and inpenetrable over the face of the water. Their accomplishment has never been exceeded. It was probably the most difficult flight ever undertaken with success. It set a precedent, and, being the first attempt, was the grandest of them all.

Both men were knighted by King George for their splendid flight. They well deserved it. In writing a brief press notice on the subject of the christening of the two pursuit planes at Camp Borden, the Department of National Defence has said:

". . . They had proved that, with a certain degree of luck, the Atlantic could be crossed by air from west to east. Many of those who later set out to prove that the direct Atlantic flight was relatively 'easy' merely proved that the element of luck still plays an important part, which is borne out by the fact that no less than sixteen lives have been lost in Atlantic flight attempts. With the comparatively recent development of the large sea-going and sea-worthy flying boat, conditions are beginning to change, and the time will come when transoceanic flights are fairly safe undertakings. At present it is not so. Alcock and Brown, while fully realizing the risk they ran, succeeded in proving the possibility of the undertaking. For that, His Majesty conferred knighthoods upon them, and for that the British Empire will ever hold their memory high."

Alcock and Brown are by no means forgotten throughout the Empire. In Canada, especially, the tenth anniversary of their epoch-making flight was celebrated in a most suitable manner. Flying clubs all over the country put on demonstration flights. At Montreal the Montreal Light Aeroplane's Club machine flew over the harbor, while, down on the river, ships of all nationalities sounded their whistles and sirens.

It has been suggested that a monument of some sort should be erected at the spot where the two daring fliers took the air at start of their long flight. The suggestion is a good one and the monument should be a good one.

A PILOT'S WIFE SPEAKING

BY NELLE F. DOOLEY

ONE reads and hears so much opposition concerning women flyers that I am prompted to write my experiences both as a pilot's sweetheart and later his wife.

Very few pilots, especially those of the old school, the army days, ever endorse the idea of women flyers; most of them are downright against it. My husband was one of the army boys, and considered by all who knew him as "an artist at the controls." He was very bitter to the idea of women invading the one thing that should be left entirely to the men—the business of being a pilot.

After his discharge from the army he was doing private flying for an independent oil company. It was there I first met him. Often I would ask him to take me up with him; always he would promise yes. But when I would go out to the field there was some reason that I could not go—the air was too bumpy, or the ship wasn't tuned up properly, or the trip was too long, it might make me sick. So the months passed and I had never "been up."

143

There were so many reasons and excuses for my not flying with him that finally I learned to be afraid of aeroplanes myself, and in the end I coaxed him to give up flying. After a year or more had passed I learned that I had committed a very grave mistake, so I wrote him and advised him to take up flying again and never leave it. This he did, and up until his death, a few months ago, I think he lived flying and dreamed flying, but never quite happy except when in the air. Incidentally, it is well to state here, that with all his years of hard flying, all the hours he had in the air, he did not die in a crash. His flying was perfect to the end.

Early one spring I coaxed a friend to take me up for a ride; he said my reaction was perfect, though he tried hard to give me a thrill so that I would forever abandon the idea of wanting to fly. He also belonged to the great army of men who do not believe women should invade the air game. This trip only made me all the more anxious, so I wrote the man, who was later to be my husband, that he must teach me to be a pilot. He promised that he would. He said that I would make a good pilot as he had watched me handle my car; that even in the most extreme crisis I never for a moment lost my head, or my sense of reasoning, that I acted first, which was the first requirement in being a successful pilot.

Last spring we were married. Then I had occasion to go on many trips with him, as he was a transport pilot on one of the large air-passenger lines through the South. On several occasions we would make solo trips. The trip had to be made, regardless of passengers, and the South is not as air-minded as it should be (though they are getting more so each day), so frequently there would be trips made sans passengers. On those occasions (he was flying one of those six-passenger monoplane types used extensively in passenger transport work) he would allow me to handle the controls to get the feel of the ship. I became quite expert at handling the ship while in the air, though of course I never tried to take-off nor land.

Later in the summer we went to Houston where he was engaged mostly in instruction work, using a small three-passenger biplane type.

Here he decided he would cure me of my desire to learn to be a pilot, so one beautiful day he took me for a long ride over the bay into Galveston, then back, following the canal that led from the deep water-way into Houston. The motor missed and trouble started. We had a forced landing in rather a bumpy pasture.

This did not seem to excite me as he had hoped it would. He soon tuned the motor off and we were ready for the take-off. He asked me if I had now had enough. I answered, "No, I am still game."

He gave me one of his smiles and we were gone. We circled over Houston, and back over the airport—there I was to learn the reason of the peculiar smile. He reached over and touched me and asked for my purse, and told me to see if my belt was securely fastened. I assured him that all was well—he gave her the gun, began to take altitude and we were off—loops, wing-turns, all the stunts, it seemed to me, he had learned during the army days. As a final dose for my benefit we spun from 2500 feet to 600 feet and then he fish-tailed me to the ground. Did I have enough?—No, it only made me all the more anxious to become a successful woman pilot.

His final admission as to my reaction in flying was that I was not emotional, I did not blow up in a crisis, and best of all that I was capable. He then went back to the only excuse a man has left concerning the average woman learning to fly—*it is not a woman's game*—it is not safe, one may never know what may happen while a ship is in the air. Of course it isn't going to happen, but if it should happen a woman has no right to be there —also, there is danger both in the take-off and in the landing for that matter; it is all right for a man to take those chances, but it is wrong for a woman to, her place is on the ground. And so ended my instructions so far as he was concerned.

If he couldn't reason with me, frighten me or coax me, he would exert his husband's authority and would refuse to take me any more. He did occasionally take me, but was always ill at ease while I was at his side. He never again took me in a biplane. When I was fortunate enough to be invited to go along, it was in a monoplane.

So to sum it all up, I think that the average pilot's reaction to a woman going into aviation is that he resents it more because he feels that it is a man's game. He feels that a woman is invading the last sacred sanctum left to man, and he uses the excuses that she is not fitted to be a pilot because of temperament and emotion.

All through the ages women have had to fight their way to reach the summit of their goal. Women going into aviation for business, as well as pleasure, and not for publicity purposes only, are going to have a harder fight than any they have yet had, but women will win. Before many years there will be any number of successful women pilots. The men will learn that even in this we have not been found lacking.

WOMEN FIND PLACE AMONG THE FLIERS

BY T. J. C. MARTYN

ALTHOUGH women have been actively identified with aviation since the earliest days of flying, more women are air pilots today than ever before, and there is every indication that still greater numbers of them will fly as aviation continues to spread its mighty wings above the earth. Today women have flown for thousands of miles, spanned whole continents and have won many races and broken many records. As pilots flying along the nation's airways, many women have proved their capabilities; as pilots looping, spinning, rolling and diving to spot landings, many have proved their skill. In aviation there is domain for women as well as for men.

The woman flier has come to be looked upon as a romantic figure. Many writers have put her on a pedestal for no other reason, apparently, than that she is a woman. Where women are concerned there seems to be a strong temptation to dramatize their exploits. Flying, itself, becomes crowned with an aurora of higher adventure and thrills. Thrills there are, of course; but they are not all the thrills of danger. Many fliers and aerial passengers have beheld the beauties of the earth from a speeding plane and have seen, too, the faerie sights which cloudland unfolds.   As in everything else, there is romance in flying, if one stops to search it out—an overwhelming appeal to the emotions and a resultant and seemingly inevitable sentimentalism.   But it is the same for women as for men; neither sex has a monopoly of appreciation for the beauties of flying; neither has a greater feeling for the subtleties of flying, nor has one necessarily more skill than the other.

Women have not taken to the air for the romance of it, at least most of them have not.   As a whole, they are an intensely practical group, some of them not more than girls.   Many of them are flying today to bring home to their sisters the joys and conveniences of air travel; they are demonstrating women's possibilities and capabilities as pilots of airplanes.   That they have done much to make other women air conscious is daily made manifest by some new aspirant to aerial honors.   There are heroines among them, as there must be; but the young woman clad in a man's breeches and riding boots, with her open-necked shirt, goggles and helmet—even if a wisp of golden hair protrudes from under it—is no darling of the gods; she is flying not so much because she is opposing men but because she has seen an opportunity for women and is demonstrating it.

Flying an airplane need not, after all, be hard work.   It has been often tested out that it is more usual to move the controls a fractional part of an inch than three inches.   There is no manual labor involved, and there is no reason whatever why women should not be just as much at home driving an airplane as they are on land driving a car or on water driving a speedboat. What is required in flying, more than anything else, is a keen and accurate judgment and a cool head and a steady hand in an emergency. Women have proved themselves to have all these qualities.

History has shown women to have had great courage, and aviation's history has been no exception. Women have flown across the Atlantic, risen miles high into the sky and stayed aloft hour after hour in light planes. These are feats that require courage. Anyone who has not taken to wings and flown out beyond the utmost purple rim of the setting sun can have no conception of the urge to descend, to get back to earth while the getting is good. To stay in the air with a thousand misgivings coursing through the mind takes courage, and women have displayed it times innumerable.

When it comes to contrasting women's ability to fly with men's, there is but one uncertainty that has not been disposed of. Women as pilots may be said to be equal in almost every way to men as pilots. They have attained a high degree of skill; they have all the necessary courage; they readily grasp all the necessary knowledge; they have all the good judgment and sensibilities to make expert pilots. Only in one respect is their ability questionable. Have women the powers of endurance in the air that men have? One notices that women have not yet broken a single record set in the same year by men; they have their own records, and in most instances, such as endurance flights, nonstop flights and high-altitude flying, they are considerably below the records set by men. Does this mean that women cannot withstand the grueling tests of meeting adversity in the air, flying through night by the aid of instruments or through fog without a sight of the ground?   Does it mean that they are fair-weather fliers?   It may be so.   And, again, it may not.

However, endurance flights have, at present, little to do with commercial aviation. No doubt the inability of women to withstand the strains and stresses of flying as well as men will inevitably disqualify them for some kinds of transport work Much transport flying is done in short hops of from 200 to 400 miles, which means from two to four hours' flying.   That is all a pilot is asked to do in one day—he is not even asked to do that day in and day out, for to do it would mean "going stale." Women, it would seem, should be able to stand such an amount of flying as is required. Some companies are indeed employing women in regular transport work and some are using them for demonstration work in a more or less general drive to enlist the sympathy and support of other women. But the number of women so employed is relatively few indeed. The reason may be the traditional prejudice against the "weaker" sex, for it is true that many men and some women dislike flying with a woman pilot for the same reason that the former hate to be shaved by a woman barber and the latter prefer a man to do their hair rather than a woman.

There is, when all is said and done, no gainsaying the fact that flying is becoming increasingly popular with women. The increase may be traced from the day when Colonel Lindbergh blazed his historic trail to Paris and focused the world's attention on aviation.   Ruth Elder led off in an attempt to be the first

woman to cross the Atlantic.   She took with her a man pilot to
do the actual flying, but credit attaches to her for the courage
she displayed in undertaking the flight.   As events turned out,
the flight was a failure, the luckless pair being forced to descend
in the open sea, but fortunately rescued by a passing ship.
Amelia Earhart, also employing a male pilot, was more successful
and succeeded in crossing the ocean in safety, thus establishing
her right to the honor of being the first woman to fly from America to Europe.   Both women are qualified pilots, and Amelia
Earhart has, since she returned from her famous flight, undertaken a tremendous amount of flying and a great deal of other
work in behalf of women and aviation.

More recently, a group of women took part in an air derby
from California to Cleveland, won by Mrs. Thaden in a little
more than twenty hours' flying time.   The race had some
high emotional moments, a number of mishaps and one regretta-
ble tragedy.   But apart from some unedifying aspects, the race
was symbolical of the part women are playing in aviation and the
keenness and enthusiasm with which they are helping in the
development of a new mode of fast travel.   Some of the women
who took part in the race are expert fliers and easily able to hold
their own with men in events which take skill rather than sus-
taining power.   Thea Rasche, a German, who has flown much in
this country, is one of the best so-called "stunt" fliers in the
world, not excepting men pilots.

The latest convert to flying is Mrs. Lindbergh, the former Anne
Morrow.   Instructed by her husband, she proved herself an able
pupil indeed, and came to her first solo flight in a great deal less

time than it takes many men. Mrs. George Kunz is another woman who flies. And there are a lot of women fliers, some well known and some whose names do not get into the newspapers. There are others who are quietly learning to fly, unnoticed by the public. Women are, according to report, often quicker to learn and more intelligent at grasping the fundamentals of flying than are a good many men. At all events, one can hardly visit a big metropolitan airport today, from New York to San Francisco, without seeing a woman fly. All this is, of course, tangible evidence of woman's growing interest in aviation.

Are we coming to a day, perhaps still far distant, when women will be as numerous in the air flying planes as they are on the surface driving cars? Today, along our congested roads one often sees a woman driving a car and sometimes one can tell a woman is driving without seeing her. One hardly ever sees a woman drive a truck, perhaps for the same reason that hardly anyone has ever seen a woman drive a locomotive. Does this mean that air women of the future will be, like their land sisters of today, the owners and drivers of their own planes? All the evidence seems to point to it. Women seem much more likely to be the users of light planes for flying over short distances to pay calls and visit over week-ends and for purely sporting purposes than they ever are likely to be transport pilots driving the great air liners of the future.

Flying, however, is itself a graceful sport, and while it may not add to a woman's charm there is nothing in it which can possibly rob her of what she has. When we all get used to flying it will be considered just as commonplace for a woman to drive a plane as it is now for her to drive a car, and women will fly, as men do, for the sheer joy of flying. Flying has a great allure. It grips the human mind and entices us up beyond the far-flung kingdom of the clouds into the crystal-clear empyrean, far away from the troubled confusion of mundane affairs. Essentially the same joys in flying appeal to women as to men; there is no sex distinction in the realm of the air.

Most of us need to escape every so often from our complicated civilization. There is no greater escape than aviation; flying is something spiritual as well as practical. The air above the earth is a new and very wonderful world, and in it woman has found a secure place.

Ground "Strafing" by
Curtiss Falcon Attack Planes

A Pursuit Squadron of
Curtiss Hawks

THE GREATEST OF ALL SPORTS

BY CLOYD P. CLEVENGER

FLYING is the king of all sports. When a man once gets the feel of the air, he would rather fly an airplane the rest of his days on coffee and doughnuts than work at anything else, even though it afforded him all the luxuries of life.

There is something about flying that gets in your system, and makes you want more of it after you once learn the art of conquering the air. Perhaps it is because flying is in reality an art in itself, and, like other arts, is a gratifying achievement. Lovers of music, literature and the other fine arts often become so engrossed in their work from the sheer satisfaction of doing it, that the monetary value placed on their efforts is of no concern to them. The greatest pleasure they get out of life is the self-satisfaction received from having created a masterpiece.

Aviation seems to have a similar enthralling atmosphere about it. Men who have dedicated their lives to its advancement have done so through the joy and satisfaction they have found in accomplishing the age-old dream of man,—to fly.

155

It was perhaps the sporting blood in Wilbur and Orville Wright, coupled with their ability as inventive geniuses, that prompted them just twenty-five years ago to build a machine which has transformed flight from a mere fantasy to a reality. And it has been the sporting element in the art of flying that has carried it on to its present-day achievements. Like many other things of modern life now accepted as vital accessories to man's way of doing things, aviation has proved its place in the commercial and industrial activities of the day.

But before its recognition as an efficient means of travel, and its acceptance by the greatest minds of the world as an important factor in the development of the industries of all nations, it passed through a wild cat, dare-devil stage. Aerial stunts took the country by storm in the early days of aviation. Plane-changing, wing-walking and a thousand other flying feats made up the programs of aerial circuses carried from one city to another by the sporting blood of the nation; and these thrills of the air met a hearty response from the general public. During these early days of flying, the big sportsmen were the promotors of aviation. Such men as August Belmont, who promoted the first aviation meet in America, brought many famous European aviators here.

Even now, as aviation is fast being woven into the commercial and industrial life of all nations, the air has lost none of its charm to those actively engaged in flying. Pilots claim that if they are out of an airplane long, they begin to get fidgety and anxious to get back into the air. There seems to be a magnetism about flying which forever holds them. Even through the starvation period of aviation, they kept on flying for the love of it and the satisfaction they got out of the "feel of the air."

Aviators say there is an artistic touch about flying, something akin to other arts, and that it is not only mental, but that there is a physical satisfaction of feeling the force of the air. If you ask a flier what he would do with a million dollars, he would tell you that he would buy a fleet of airplanes, like a horseman would establish a stable of thoroughbreds, and then just do nothing but fly over the country.

Most men in all walks of life have hobbies. With some it is horses or athletics; others find their greatest relaxation in hunting or fishing; and there are still others whose greatest joy comes from the pleasure of either piloting a plane or enjoying the air from the passenger compartment.

Many club men of various cities now use airplanes to travel to and from their country clubs. They can attend to their business up to the very last minute, and then, with no discomfort whatever, step into a cabin plane and fly out to their club.

One of the greatest handicaps to big game hunting today is the barrier of distance between the business centers and the hunting spots in the mountains. The most inaccessible places are now easily reached by airplane, and with considerably less fatigue than by auto or train, because there is always a spot somewhere near the hunting ground to land. In places covered by lakes, the sportsman takes a trip in a seaplane. Over the ocean, schools of fish can be "spotted" from the air; then the flying fisherman drops down to the surface of the water and casts his line from the plane.

So, with the advancement of the greatest of all means of travel now rigidly fixed as a safe, secure and speedy means of transportation, a trend of sportsmanship has led the way. The great airlines fast being established throughout the nations are merely following in the wake of the sportman's pleasure.

THE STORY OF FLIGHT

A BRIEF REVIEW OF MAN'S ACHIEVEMENT IN THE AIR

IN the story of flight, more perhaps than in any other conquest made by man, we see the romance in man's struggles to subdue the universe outside him by the aid of the science and faith within.

Near the Olympia, in South Kensington Museum of Science, reposes the clumsy vehicle with which man, after centuries of hope and endeavor, achieved the first true flight. In that historic structure of stick and wire and linen, the Wright Brothers flew on the red-letter day of December 17, 1903, a distance of 852 feet, their flight lasting 59 seconds, during which they reached a speed short of 20 m.p.h., little more than a man's height from the ground.

Today* the speed record is nearly six miles a minute, the duration record is almost three days, the height record stands at over seven miles, the distance record is little short of 5,000 miles.

In the Exhibition itself will be seen machines that in the course of their military and commercial duties can achieve speeds

*August, 1929.

159

of 200 m.p.h., heights of five miles, distances without descending of three thousand miles, durations of fifty hours.

And in the long struggle whose first victory was that stick and wire structure, culminating in the swift winged shapes of today with their mighty power-plants, is written the history of flight. It is a history in which all nations have played their part.   Italy, with the foresight and mighty breadth of vision of that world-figure, Leonardo da Vinci, first to see flight as a mechanical problem.   Britain, with Sir George Cayley, Wenham and String-fellow, who grappled with the outstanding technical problems long before success was in sight.   Germany, with the practical experience and theoretical grasp of Lilienthal, earliest martyr of the faith.   France, with Ader and Le Bris, the precursors, and Voison and Bleriot, the contemporaries of the Wrights.   And finally, to America, the glory of the Wrights' final achievement and, hardly less glorious, the near achievement of Langley.

And hardly less important than the work of those great historic figures, is the work of countless others who followed after, whose names a brief history's crowded scroll has no space to record.   The chemists whose knowledge has created compounds of amazing strength and lightness, and engineers whose knowledge and experience have fashioned it into shapes safe and economical; the scientists, who have tracked down in laboratory and wind tunnel the mysterious laws of the air; the designers, whose final conception has risen from their labors—a machine entity; and last, but not least, the pilot, by whom the machine is judged and justified, whose skill and daring so often launched it on the air when knowledge was scant and doubters many.

So early arose the desire for flight, so old the progenitors of the designer and pilot of today, that the earliest pioneers are almost mythical figures. The next stage of the story is the coming of early and unpractical theorists. Then begins the era of those who, though still wandering in an unscientific mist, yet realized that a solution of the problem could come only with laborious and frequent experiment. Then for a time flying effort was directed up a blind alley, that of non-dirigible sustentation. The end of the eighteenth century saw the development of the balloon, but man, his appetite whetted by a taste for the possibilities of victory, retraced his steps; returned to the basic, the theoretical problems of flight. Paucton (1784), a French mathematician, followed by Launoy and Bienvenu, worked out the theory of the helicopter. Meerwin of Karlsruhe calculated the wing area necessary to sustain a man. Sir George Cayley (1774-1875) devoted his life to a study of the first principles of flight, and helped to lay the foundations of aerodynamics. His name, said M. Alphonse Berget, must be written "in letters of gold" at the beginning of the history of the aeroplane. Henson, Maxim and Stringfellow constructed large models, power-driven, that actually flew, and Wenham's classic lecture on the possibilities of flight to the Aeronautical Society was the inspiration of their efforts.

So much for the theory. Other pioneers, working on different lines, saw first that the theory must be tested by practice; secondly, that to master the air would need a high degree of skill and knowledge even with the most soundly constructed flying machine. These were the gliders, who first rode the air in heavier-than-air machines—like the balloonists, not controlling it, but at least not entirely at its mercy.   Le Bris, a French sea captain, was the first.   Next came Otto Lilienthal, born in 1848, who, after years of study of the theoretical basis of flight and many small experiments, launched in 1891 his first glider, and made over 2,000 experimental glides in different machines before his fatal accident in 1896.   But other gliders in England and America carried on the great tradition, while the twentieth century, which was to see the solution of the problem, dawned and waxed.

Other inventors there were who went straight from a theoretical investigation and model experiments to the actual finished machine.   Thus Adolphe Penaud, a brilliant young Frenchman, with an apparently instinctive knowledge of the principles of flight, constructed models that flew and later, a full-size aeroplane which, given a modern engine, might have flown. Hargraves in Australia, in a series of extended experiments, stumbled upon the invention of the box kite in 1893.

Clement Ader, in France, after a series of courageous efforts, built the "Avion," about whose actual leaving of the ground in 1897 there is still dispute.   His machine is commemorated in the French word for aeroplane, "avion."

Finally, greatest perhaps of all these early pioneers, essentially and absolutely modern in spirit, is Professor Samuel Langley.   Langley was a distinguished American scientist who, after a successful career in other sciences, devoted years of careful and methodical study to the laws of aerodynamics.   By means of a whirling arm and other laboratory experiments, he reduced vague speculations to exact mathematical formulae, and, in 1896, in a large model aeroplane, fitted with a light steam engine, made a series of flights, one of which exceeded three-quarters of a mile.   Later, at the request of the War Office, he made a full-scale aeroplane, with a radial engine designed by Manly, the power-weight ratio of which was not approached for many years after.

The actual flights were attempted in 1903, but were unsuccessful in each case owing to the wreck of the machine in launching; the pilot, Manly, escaped uninjured.   This machine, with minor modifications, was flown by Glenn Curtiss in 1914.

In spite of Langley's great achievement it should not be considered, as it so often is, that only bad luck robbed him of victory.   He had genius, science, perseverance; but he saw flying as a scientific problem.   He had not the fondness of flying for flying's sake.   No element of the pilot was included in his "make-up."

This was the final secret of the Wrights' triumph.   They united the patient, theoretical groping of the scientist, the experienced empiricism of the engineer, the adaptability and imagination of the inventor, and the practical and enlightened skill of the pilot.   They started—helped certainly by the knowledge of Langley and other pioneers—from the very beginning. Assuring themselves of the basic facts with model experiments, they turned to gliders, and made innumerable gliding flights to learn the secrets of control.   Then, that being learned, and not until then, they set about designing and fitting to their evolved glider an engine and propellers.

On the morning of December 17, 1903, between the

hours of 10:30 o'clock and noon, four flights were made, two by Orville Wright and two by Wilbur. On that historic morning, five spectators were present on the draughty field at Kitty Hawk, North Carolina, and watched the Wrights' frail structure battle with a 25 m.p.h. wind. Then, as the Wrights laconically said, when they were satisfied that "the machine possessed sufficient power to fly, sufficient strength to withstand the shocks of landings, and sufficient capacity of control to make flight safe in boisterous winds as well as in calm air . . . we at once packed our goods and returned home, knowing that the age of the flying machine had come at last."

Of the days that followed that dawn, only the briefest outline can be written. While the Wrights labored to perfect their machine, independent experiments were proceeding apace. Ferber, joined by Voisin and Archdeacon, drew slowly nearer success. Santos Dumont, the brilliant young Brazilian, made the first heavier-than-air flight in Europe in October, 1906. In the next year Henry Farman made short flights, and in 1908 Wilbur Wright arrived in Europe to demonstrate his machine. In 1909, Bleriot amazed Europe by his crossing of the Channel, and the great Rheims Meeting in the same year aroused an enthusiasm worthy of the achievement that had come to fruition.

During the period, 1909 to 1914, man slowly developed the potentialities of his invention. Step by step performances went up, and the types slowly became standardized. Aerodynamics began to take shape as a science, aircraft engineering as a branch of engineering. Such pioneers as A. V. Roe, Sopwith, Curtiss, Pelterie, Morane, Cody and Deperdussin worked steadily and brilliantly on different lines of progress. The float seaplane, the flying boat and the amphibian emerged. By the beginning of the war period the aeroplane had become definitely a practical vehicle.

The war period took the designs as they were at its beginning and developed the military features of each to undreamed-of refinements. Performance figures shot up like rockets, theories went by the board, production methods underwent a revolution. Men woke up almost overnight to find in the aeroplane the most highly finished form of locomotion men had ever had.

Came peace, and men saw that more difficult than the task of re-erecting the destroyed was that of adapting the created— to beat the temper of the sword to the ruggedness of the plough-share. To tame the aeroplane, to adapt the high-powered thunderbolt of war to the uses of peace and commerce—that was the task about which the post-war world set itself. Designers evolved machines suitable for peace, two-seaters for the ordinary man, giant twenty-seaters as argosies of the air, economic to operate, safe and fast. Progress did not stop. Range, endurance, reliability, speed, safety, climb, and efficiency increased by leaps, and still show no sign of halting. Aircraft operators laid out a network of air lines over Europe, gradually stretching tentacles down to Egypt and India, over Africa, Australia and America. Pilots, too, performed feats that dazzled the world, blazing the trail for the air routes that were to follow after them. Slowly the world woke up to the fact that aviation was now a normal vehicle of life. Ordinary men and women, not supermen, learned to fly their own machines at British flying clubs in a few hours, letters passed as a matter of course along American air mail routes, German citizens traveled from town to town by air as formerly by rail.

"Transport," a great writer has said, "is the essence of civilization." The coracle, the sailing ship, the steamship on sea, and the chariot, the stagecoach, the train, and the motor car on land, marked the progress of civilization through transports of increasing speed and mobility. Last of all came the aeroplane, ignoring the distinctions of land and water, road and jungle and desert, the fastest vehicle man has ever produced. It is to fulfill that conception of the aeroplane that designers have labored and whose success is plain in the commercial machines of to-day.

With this new conception, came to an end the first aerial age. The first age saw the invention and development of the aeroplane as a machine. To-day marks the dawn of the second aerial age, the development of the aeroplane—not as just a machine—but as an integral part of the life of the community. The layman who views aircraft of a performance and safety which would have been incredible ten years ago, the very conception of which would have been impossible twenty years before that, must necessarily ask, "What of the Future?"

And here the experts one and all agree that we shall see a development to which our imagination hardly dares set a limit. We have flying boats now capable of seating twenty or more people. But the flying boats of the future, the great trans-oceanic air lines of tomorrow, will seat five times that number in their capacious hulls. At present the limit of man's height above the surface of the earth is conditioned by the atmosphere, which grows rarer and rarer with the miles, till at last it will support the wing no longer, nor yield grip to the propeller, air to the engine, or oxygen to the occupant. There are devices whereby engine and man are fed, the one by superchargers, the other by oxygen apparatus, to reach heights otherwise unattainable. It is only a step further, a development of lines already embarked upon, to the hermetically sealed cabin machine with variable wings and propellers, which will fly at heights at present unreached and—owing to the decreased air pressure—at speeds four or five times that of the lower regions. Then we shall see 300 m.p.h. passenger-carrying craft making the New York-Paris journey in a day, and great lines linking up the two hemispheres and the Temperate, Tropic and Arctic zones.

Nor is it difficult to see the day when the aeroplane, if not combined with the car, is at least as common a possession. Already the two-seater airplane is cheaper than many cars, and in the days to come, when production methods expand, it should become at least as cheap as the cheapest. As long as men think in terms of their own country, and a voyage outside it as a rare occasional venture, so long, it is true, the aeroplane will not reach its highest development. But as men think and live more and more internationally, so will the aeroplane become more and more the appropriate vehicle. For it expresses two of the increasingly important factors in modern life—disregard of boundaries and limitations, and the desire for speed.

Just as surely as man will progress in the future, aviation will just as surely progress with him.

THE PASSING OF PIONEER DAYS

BY RAY LITTLE

Ray Little, the author of this article, was one of the original band of Army pilots who pioneered the air mail service with surplus Army planes. He later joined the Boeing System when it took over the transcontinental air mail contract. Little flew the first eastbound mail plane from San Francisco in September, 1920, and, after nine years, he is still flying the mail. More recently he flew the first eastbound "Night Transcontinental" out of San Francisco. His regular flight now is on the tri-motored twelve-passenger transports, which are flown at night over the Sierra Mountains.

Little has thus engaged in flying from the early, uncertain and more adventurous days down to the present when air transport has become a thoroughly systematized business proposition. In this article he relates a pilot's impression of the changes that have taken place.

A PILOT used to go out all buckled up like a warrior looking for battle. Now he is a professional man with his suit pressed. On the tri-motors I do not even have a flying suit. Parachutes are left in the hangar. A transport pilot, hooded and belted, is beginning to look like a

168

Don Quixote. There is now little more adventure in flying a transport plane than there is in running a street car.

When a job is comparatively safe there is no more adventure in it. Daredevils of the air, like the bronco busters of the West, exist only in the movies and the thrill magazines. The air trail blazing is largely done—in this country.

Flying is rapidly passing out of the pioneer stage. Like all other adventurers into new and strange realms, the early fliers led the way, a host of followers came, and the romance began to disappear. When enough people are familiar with air travel, there will be no more mystery about it. We are rapidly approaching the day when there will be no more excitement about flying than there is about railroading.

This condition is being brought about by numerous aids to flight, aircraft improvements, and development of airways.

One year ago the pilot was his own general, making his decisions on his own judgment alone. Today he receives the advice of a corps of weather observers, and the orders of ground superintendents by radio telephone—not in code but in spoken words. Directive radio, by dots and dashes, tells him when he is off his course.

Two years ago there were practically no marked airways except the old transcontinental. The pilot had to be skilled in reading maps to find his way about. Today a flier is aided by the signs on roofs and fields. Two years ago there were practically no lighted airways. Cross-country planes had to stop at night, except on the Transcontinental and a few other trips. Today the nation is rapidly becoming a web of chain lights at night.   It is as easy to find one's way at night, in clear weather, as in the daytime.   Airways are lighted and maintained by the Department of Commerce, not for the air mail contractors alone, but for all who wish to use them.   The intermediate fields, weather reports and radio service are free to all.   The other night I flew a Boeing tri-motor over the Sierras, between 8 P. M. and 10 P. M., and my load of passengers acted as if it were a moonlight auto ride.   Passengers are steadily becoming more casual about flying.

Nine years ago we had nothing but airplanes and these were not too good.   The Army planes with which we began flying the mail in 1918 would carry about 400 pounds, in addition to pilot and fuel.   Those ships were equipped with 400-horsepower engines.   Our present planes, the Boeing 40-A for example, with its 525-horsepower Hornet, carry as much as 1,600 pounds. On that basis, we have increased the efficiency of commercial planes several hundred per cent in ten years.

Airplanes used to be hard to handle.   A man never took off in one of the old type without a vague feeling that it might be his last flight.   Now we think nothing of it—any more than we worry about riding in our cars.

Think, for example, of Burr Winslow, who has flown over the Sierra Nevada "Hump" between Reno and San Francisco Bay about 2,000 times.   And he's had only one forced landing. Winslow, like all other transport pilots, makes flying his business, nothing more.   If I am not mistaken, Winslow is somewhat bored with his job at times, just as you may be bored with your routine job, whatever it is.   Clair Vance has done it 1,900 times.

I wouldn't quit flying—I like it.   But I do feel that all these improvements and safety measures have taken most of the adventure out of the business.   Formerly, when a man went out to take his run, he was armored for a tilt.   He chatted in an over-jubilant way with his fellow fliers—much as the Musketeers must have done.   Three or four men, holding hands like whip-crackers, took a run at your propeller.   Maybe the motor started.   Maybe the prop struck someone—as often happened.   Then you took off in a great cloud of dust, with all the field force and half the town as observers.   Those old ships would fly all right, and they had speed.   But you didn't know what might happen.

Some of the most dramatic events of any pioneer era happened along the old Transcontinental.   To fly alone over an ocean of black fog at night, with no idea where he was, no communication—nothing but a couple of flares and a parachute—was not exactly like attending afternoon tea.

A flier in the old days was in life, clear up to the hilt.   I remember when some fellow in the Army discovered what caused a tail spin, and how to stop it.   Many men had died in tail spins.   The action of a plane in a spin was mysterious, like the disappearance of ships on the sea in the times of the explorers.   Some uncanny power seemed to take the machine out of the pilot's control.   Now there are some types of plane that you cannot make spin, and there is no commercial plane that will spin voluntarily.

Well, the Forty-niners and the cowboys had their day, and it looks like we air vets have about had ours.   It must make an old cowman mad to see a fellow in shiny boots and polo pants riding a slick horse.   Well, it hurts, in a way, to see these Boeing pilots climbing up into heated cabins, wearing business suits and straw hats, and talking to somebody over the 'phone all the way over the run.   Next there will be a demand for telephones in the passenger cabins too, so the travelers can call up their offices, for this can be done today with our radiophone system now being completed by the Boeing System between San Francisco Bay and Chicago.

Well, you might say they are making flying safe for everybody, which is what the country wanted.   A few people want thrills, but they want safe thrills.   Some don't want any thrills at all; they want to go places in a hurry.   I am glad that the new flying era is here.

BEFORE EVERYBODY CAN FLY

*Mechanical Difficulties and Legal Tangles Which Must be
Solved if the Family Plane is to Take the Place
of the Automobile for Business and Pleasure*

MOST everyone has heard the common prophecy that very soon the person of small income will have the pleasure of choosing between a road "flivver" and an equally safe, cheap and easy-to-operate aeroplane.

That day has practically arrived as far as first cost is concerned, but there is a long series of mechanical difficulties to be overcome, to say nothing of legal tangles and perhaps a few riots and rebellions, before the human race takes to the air in swarms.

In the first place, there is the human equation. Any moron who could tell his right hand from his left and see 100 feet ahead was considered competent to drive a horse and wagon in the good old days. The first automobile licenses were obtainable for the asking and paying of a fee, regardless of intelligence or eyesight. Nowadays nearly all the states require tests showing at least some degree of fitness to sit behind the wheel. This has barred out a good many and soon will exclude more.

The men and women physically and mentally capable of learning to be reasonably safe fliers form a still smaller class, though once in the air an up-to-date plane is easier to drive than a car. It is more like a buggy. The thing flies itself. But skill and judgment are required for getting on and off the ground, even when everything is all right.

Still higher ability is demanded when engine failure or other trouble calls for a forced landing. For every foot of height, the average plane can coast with dead engine five feet horizontally, which gives the aviator considerable latitude in picking an empty field. However, at best, it is a real emergency, far different from parking a car along the roadside and telephoning to the nearest garage.

The bulk of the population is crowding into the cities, where ordinances have already forbidden flying below certain heights. These "ceilings" are supposed to be high enough so that in case of motor trouble the aviator will have no difficulty in coasting down to some open field outside the city limits or dropping into the river or ocean, and at least not breaking any pedestrian's neck.

This at once reveals one of the weak spots in the optimistic notion that soon all city buildings will have landing fields on their roofs. How are they going to land or rise without getting below that "ceiling"? And if a motor "conks" just as a plane has left one of the roofs, what can it do but pitch down into the crowded street?

Before anything of the kind is permitted, someone will have to perfect a motor as sure not to stop unexpectedly as a good watch. Besides this the planes, instead of the present roaring public nuisances, must become as quiet as the average automobile; otherwise the cities would be madhouses for everyone but the deaf.   People who live in the vicinity of airports have learned to their sorrow what the noise does to property values.

Even with silent planes and infallible motors, will office workers learn not to be distracted by the incessant flickering shadows from broad wings passing overhead?   The great military powers are experimenting with transparent wing fabrics, which may be the answer for peace as well as war.

Even when all objections to the machine itself have been met, it is evident that there will be a grand division of the goats from the sheep—many goats who are only permitted to fly in the country and a few sheep licensed to fly into town.

If the skyscraper tops are to be utilized as flying fields, it will mean planes swarming like gnats over the cities during the rush hours, requiring 100 per cent perfection of police regulation. If any two of the swarm collide, the pair will have no chance of gliding away to the outskirts, but must crash wherever fate takes them—perhaps in the midst of a matinee crowd just leaving a theater.

When, however, all these bothersome questions have been ironed out, the roof-top perch for flying machines may well be the solution of city street traffic congestion.   Already experiments are being made for a roof-landing field that can be revolved so that planes will always take off in the face of the wind.   This field is a platform, 210 feet long by 60 feet wide, and besides being revolvable, can be tipped as much as 25 degrees from the horizontal.

In landing, the plane runs up the incline, and is further

retarded by spring cables, while powerful suction fans prevent it from bouncing.   In taking off, the plane starts from the top of the incline, thus having the aid of gravity in gaining speed. Also it can use the battleship catapult.

The fundamental weakness of the aeroplane, of course, is that it does not fly like the bird, but planes or skims, depending on speed.   The faster it goes, the better the pilot's control. At 90 miles an hour and up it controls itself, but at the critical moment of landing it must still do about 40 to be manageable. If an aviator tried to land at 10 miles an hour he would land on his nose or his ear.

Ducks and some other heavy water birds take off and land in almost as clumsy a fashion, but the majority can fly straight up, drop straight down to a slender twig without a jar, and hover almost motionless in mid-air.   Some success has been achieved with the helicopter, a flying machine with revolving wings, and the ornithopter, whose wings flap.   Mechanically there is nothing to prevent perfecting these designs to a point where they can hover above a landing, waiting their turn to drop straight down to the exact spot assigned to them.

Then, indeed, will the problem of commuting by air to the city have been met.   Flying home in the evening, the city worker will hover over his home, blowing his horn for his wife to step into the private hangar and pull the counterweights, which will cause the roof to open up like a drawbridge, permitting the machine to gently drop in.

If the "missis" is out or busy on the telephone, he can light in the front yard, get out, pull the roof open himself, go back and hop in. Or, of course, the family hangar may be on the roof of the bungalow itself. No doubt inventive minds will set to work on schemes by which the home-coming flier can pull the latchstring of his roof from the air.

The cost of flying, for the average man, is surprisingly close to that of running an automobile. The price range of the planes, complete, would probably be from $2,000 to $7,000. But he can get a complete plane for as low as $695—no more than an equipped flivver—with a motorcycle engine and a 23-foot wing span. This machine might perhaps be a bit difficult and tricky for the average man to fly.

So he might buy a certain two-seater biplane for $1,900. Its wing span is 28 feet, its length overall 22 feet, it is 6 feet high, carries a 375-pound load, weighs 800 pounds, has an 80-horse-power engine, has 85 miles an hour high speed, 75 miles cruising speed, and 46 miles landing speed. It climbs 560 feet a minute at sea level, can fly as high as 15,000 feet, carries 15 gallons of fuel, has a 375-mile range, burns 3 gallons of fuel an hour at cruising speed, uses stick control, is equipped with shock absorbers and is approved by the Department of Commerce.

Or he might buy this four-passenger cabin monoplane for $6,950; engine of 110 horsepower, 41:6 feet wing span, 26:3 feet overall, 7:9 feet high, carries 990 pounds of load, weighs 1,510 pounds, has 110 miles an hour speed, 90 miles cruising speed and 46 miles landing speed, climbs 500 feet a minute at sea level and has a ceiling of 16,000. It carries 42 gallons of gas, has a range of 500 miles, burns seven gallons of gas per hour at cruising speed, has dual stick control, brakes and shock absorbers, and is approved by the Department of Commerce.

Between the two planes just described there are some thirty-four types on the market from which the average man may select. He can get in a good deal of flying in demonstrations alone!

The aeroplane burns a high test gasoline which costs more than ordinary automobile fuel, of course, and labor charges are probably higher. But by using a public landing field, with hangar and service facilities, the average man can operate his aeroplane, including insurance, depreciation, gas, oil, service and repairs, for as low as 18 to 20 cents a mile, the Aeronautical Chamber of Commerce asserts. With a $4,000 plane, say, and doing a good deal of flying, he can count on a maintenance charge of about $2,000 a year.

The number of private fliers is already high and is growing daily. There are now 4,844 licensed pilots in the United States, and 3,000 privately owned planes.

Colonel Lindbergh is, of course, the greatest private flier on earth, and does more actual flying than even many transport pilots. In 1928 he flew 65,000 miles, was aloft 800 hours, and carried 1,500 passengers.

There are 200 private owners near New York City. In the Wall Street district alone there are 39 men who fly their own planes. Salesmen, doctors, commuters, ranchers, planters, use planes for work as well as sport. In the New York City area 20 business men fly their own seaplanes or amphibians—mostly for commuting purposes. Flying fields are becoming more common every year. California has the greatest number, followed by New York, Illinois and Michigan.

The chief obstacle for the private flier today is the landing field, a large area of level ground without high surrounding obstructions, something that only the wealthy can afford. But there are so many public landing fields that the average man can own his own plane and keep it in a public hangar at a cost no greater than that of maintaining an automobile in a public garage. There are 1,400 landing fields in the United States with hangars and service facilities such as gasoline, oil and mechanics. And there are 4,000 other fields without such facilities where the private flier may land if forced to.

The latest development for private flying is the formation of clubs. A group of people band together and share the cost of field, planes, etc. In Jackson Heights, a suburb of New York City, a group of moderately well-to-do people combined, bought a cabin monoplane, and maintain it jointly at an airport. The plane has a lavatory and kitchenette and a radio, and the club members hold dances and dinners high in the air.

Then there are air country clubs, where golf links and tennis courts are maintained with the landing field. Such clubs have been established in Westchester County, New York, in New Jersey, at Newport, R. I., and around San Francisco and Los Angeles, California. Other aviation country clubs are rapidly being formed and are organized with reciprocal privileges as yacht clubs.

TRAINING A THOUSAND AIR STUDENTS

BY DONALD M. EWING

TRAINING one student or a score of students for aeronautical work is an easy matter—a one-man job, in fact. But training a thousand students is immensely more difficult. It is an undertaking so extensive that it can be accomplished successfully only with 100 per cent equipment, 100 per cent personnel, and 100 per cent organization.

An interesting example of such comprehensive enterprise is that of the Universal Aviation Schools. Universal is operating ten schools in important cities throughout the Middle West, covering every branch of aviation training.

At the head of the Universal Aviation Schools is Willis B. Haviland, who was a Lieutenant Commander in the Navy during the war, and who previously had served with the Lafayette Escadrille, having received numerous decorations and citations for acts of bravery.

Haviland, with his assistants, is directly responsible for the development of the operating plan of Universal schools. Under this system each school has a complete organization of its own,

Kelly Field, Texas
The Advanced Training
Center

Brooks Field
San Antonio, Texas

March Field
Riverside
California

identical with that of each of the other schools. Haviland's efforts tend chiefly toward direction of the schools as a whole, and toward formulating and putting into effect various policies decided on.

He is, of course, directly under the officials of Universal Aviation Corporation—Dan W. Jones, president, and Colonel Halsey Dunwoody, executive vice-president. Universal Aviation Corporation is a unit in the Aviation Corporation, one of the principal big groups in the aeronautic industry. These connections provide the Universal schools a financial foundation, which is invaluable in building up the sort of organization required in this work.

An extensive system for enrolling new students has been established by the Universal schools. This part of the organization is divided into two groups—sales by personal contact, and sales through advertising and use of the mails. The former is in charge of J. G. Lamb, and the latter is handled by William Dings. Lamb formerly was sales manager for Universal's school at Minneapolis. Dings, who is officially known as registrar of the schools, formerly managed the Robertson Flying School at St. Louis, which is now controlled by Universal.

Under Lamb the organization chart extends, for enrollment purposes, right down into each individual school. At each school there is a sales manager, and under him are numerous salesmen. It is the local sales manager's problem to keep his organization producing at all times; it is Lamb's job to see that these local sales managers are keeping up the enrollments.

To keep the routine moving rapidly and smoothly, an extensive system of handling inquiries has been established. A corps of trained letter readers is kept busy every day opening inquiries. These are carefully analyzed and classified according to the type of information desired—whether the applicant wants to take up flying, wishes to be a mechanic, desires to learn the business side of aviation, or is considering a welding course. Each applicant is given individual attention, and every effort is made to treat his query as a distinct and individual problem. When a student who obviously should not be in aviation seeks to enroll, a frank letter is written giving the reasons why it is thought he should seek some other vocation.

In the actual training side of Universal schools, Paul Paine is supervisor of ground schools. He and Haviland collaborate in working out the general ground pattern, with Captain R. D. Hughes as a liaison man to co-ordinate flight and ground instruction.

Under these men are the individual schools, each with a manager who, in turn, works in co-operation with a corps of experts in various branches of aviation training. The schools are located at several important airports in order that the student may choose in which part of the country he prefers to be located while in training; whether he desires to live during the training period in a small or a large city, etc.

The first school to be started was at Minneapolis, where Trevor Williams, who is a veteran war pilot, is manager and also in charge of Universal Aviation Corporation's affairs in the central northwest. Because he also has this latter duty, Williams has V. L. Jones, an old-time pilot and barnstormer, as active director of the ground school there. Two schools also under direct supervision of the Minneapolis headquarters have been opened near by—one at Rochester, Minnesota, and one at St. Paul.

The second of the Universal schools was that at St. Louis, now in charge of William P. McFail, for eight years one of the country's leading pilots and the pilot of the first ship on the Universal Air Lines. At Marion, Illinois, is another school under Allen Hagerty. One of the best-known Universal schools is at Kansas City; it is known as the Porterfield Flying School and was only recently acquired by Universal. It was founded by E. E. Porterfield, head of the American Eagle Aircraft Corporation, and now is under Captain L. A. Miller, who earned his wings during the war. Farther west is a Universal school at Oklahoma City, Oklahoma, under Ray Kutterer, a Universal graduate, who completed his training a few years ago. At Wichita is another school, founded by E. A. Watkins, president of the Central Air Lines, now a Universal subsidiary, with George MacDonald in charge. Still another Universal school is located in Memphis, Tennessee, with Captain Lloyd Juelson as manager. The farthest east of the Universal schools is the one at Cleveland, Ohio, where David R. McCauley is in charge. McCauley is a well-known pilot and was borrowed temporarily from Universal by the Guggenheim Fund for the Promotion of Aeronautics to conduct experiments in blind flying.

In each of these schools, identical instruction is given, and complete, modern flying and ground equipment is used. The standard power equipment consists of the most modern air-cooled engines. All of the old water-cooled jobs have been cast aside except a few that are retained for ground mechanical instruction and a few of the OX-5 type, which are likely to be in use in small ships for a few more years, though considered obsolete for advanced commercial work.

Tri-motored equipment also is used in the schools, two Fords being available for the advanced training. Numerous types of cabin ships are available, in addition to the regular small training planes.

Largely because of the efficiency of training in these schools, Universal recently was granted insurance on students while learning to fly. These schools were perhaps the first in the United States to receive such coverage. Previously a student had always been looked on as too great a risk for insurance, but after careful study, a well-known firm of underwriters offered Universal a blanket policy, stating that they were satisfied Universal's system is sufficiently thorough and advanced to eliminate most of the risk involved in training its students. The cost of this insurance is only $20 for $1,000, covering life and disability, and $45 for $2,500.

Eight courses are offered in the Universal schools, as follows:

Pilots' ground course, qualifying for Department of Commerce private pilot's license.

Limited commercial course, qualifying for Department of Commerce limited commercial license.

Transport pilots' course, covering every type of flying and qualifying the student to apply for a transport pilot's license.

Day ground mechanics' course, covering six weeks of intensive mechanical study both in the classroom and in actual work at an airport.

Night mechanics' course, given at downtown buildings in larger cities, not as intensive as the day course, but adequate for men working at other positions in the daytime.

Aviation welding course, also given at downtown laboratories; one of the most popular and unusual of aviation courses offered by the Universal schools.

Aviation business course, covering twenty lectures on all phases of aviation business, each given by a well-known expert in his particular field. Universal was the first in the country to start aviation business courses.

"We have tried to create a school system that is smooth and efficient in each of the three components which are so necessary to success—equipment, personnel and organization," said Mr. Haviland, in commenting on the Universal line-up. "It has taken time to do it, but I believe we have succeeded. The greatest need in aviation today is for experienced personnel and we are seeking to supply that need. Especially is this need found in the business end of the industry. Some years ago we had the idea that the man to fill an aviation executive position had to have been a good pilot. Now we realize that the executive must have two qualifications, executive ability and aviation ability. Neither is sufficient of itself. In other words, an engineman on a train may know everything in the world about running a train, but be a total loss at running a division of a railroad. There is a big field in aviation today—an unfilled field. No school can conscientiously guarantee to place all of its men. But we do

everything we can to get jobs for our men.   Naturally some men
show inaptitude in an aviation school, just as some do in their
college work, but those who show that they are really good
material usually find jobs without much difficulty.

LIFE OF A FLYING CADET

BY CAPTAIN F. I. EGLIN
U. S. Army Air Corps, Brooks Field

M ARCH 1st. July 1st. November 1st. Suitcases, large and small; "city clothes;" mustaches.

Fifteen minutes later: shaved lips, coveralls, upperclassmen, inspections. Drill, and more drill. Barracks, bunk, and bull. Confusion. "Dodo."

Different types, different accents, different ideas.

Flying cadets assembled, to enter into an entirely new and troubled existence. Gone, the old life, the office work, the days of leisure and freedom, the nights beneath the summer moon, old friends, old loves. In its place, a life of ceaseless activity, of hurry and work and worry, of feverish excitement. A mad, nervous existence, in which neither love nor leisure nor peace has any place.

Who will forget those first two weeks? Examinations, drill— drill, examinations. The orientator, the "609", the complex co-ordinator, the psychological, Ruggles pursuit, Schneiders, esophoria. Reaction time, double time, squad right and to the rear. The quarter mile at reveille. Inspections from 6:00 A. M. to 10:00 P. M. One bell after another. No time to wash—

187

never a minute's rest. When you are not drilling, you are standing inspections. When you are not standing inspections, you walk tours. Gigs—more gigs.

Bunk flying, awake or asleep. Incessant chatter. No sleep. Dreams. Getting up before daylight. Confusion, nerves and work—always work.

Drill. Squad east and west. Double time. To the rear. March. Watching the PT's do rolls at a thousand feet. Will you ever fly—or is it just a dream? "ATTENTION." "Pull your shoulders back, Mister Dumbjohn. You are at attention." "What's your name, Mister?" "Do you understand?" "Yes, SIR." There's an upper-classman who must have been a top kick at some disciplinary barracks. Who said this was a flying school anyway? Or have you enlisted in the Infantry?

Examinations. Three times to the orientator. Innumerable trips to the School of Aviation Medicine. More bunk flying. Blood pressure 130—14 on your "Schneider recheck," on *what?* You put the line of light across the light. If you don't, you have hydrophobia. Worry. Grief. Apprehension.

But finally the two weeks drag to an end, and you draw helmets and goggles. Flying starts on Monday. Could it be true? Would the weather be fair?

Monday finally comes, and you march to "A" Stage for your first hop. The talk by the Stage Commander—will he never stop! Who has ever seen a "T" before? You meet your instructor, adjust your parachute and have your first ride. Fifteen minutes of joy. Fifteen minutes of pleasure. Sunshine and clouds. The sky is blue. One, two, three thousand feet. The

hangars are only a marker for the field. The ship levels off.
Back comes the throttle and, "Follow me through these banks."
The ship banks and turns right, then left. Level again. Again
the throttle comes back. You feel the stick being shaken.
"You try that." Three thousand feet, and your first time on the
controls. You move the stick and rudder cautiously. The
plane banks—and slips. Something new—the orientator had
not acted that way. You notice that the nose is not swinging
as it should. The instructor is patting the side of his helmet.
You think a minute. The plane keeps slipping. Oh, yes!
You give left rudder. Too much—the plane stops slipping and
skids instead. The instructor pats the other side of his head
and you take off a little rudder. There! The plane turns
correctly at last. After repeating this a few times you wonder
if you will ever learn to fly.

But after a while you seem to be doing better. You start
landings. And then, the anxious days before SOLO.

One after another your classmates solo. Two in one day—
one on the next. Occasionally one is checked—anxious hours for
him—elimination. You wonder if you will be eliminated too.
Then one day, after you have made several good landings, and
your turns, spins and forced landings have been fair, the instructor unfastens his safety belt, turns around and asks you for a
cigarette. You know what is coming, and you search frantically,
wondering if he will change his mind. Finally you find one.
Then, "Do you think you can take it around?" Do you! Well
————! But all you say is, "Yes, sir." "All right. Go ahead
and watch out for the traffic."

The first solo. Even a bigger kick than the first ride. Half afraid—half confident. You look around carefully; clean your goggles. Your first and maybe your last. You give her the gun and take off. The plane seems so light. The nose is too high or too low. Finally you have it level. You wonder if you can take it around without hitting someone. In fact, where did all the planes come from anyway? You have never noticed so many in the air at one time before—and all going in the same direction as you wanted to go. First turn—slipped a little and skidded a little but made it. Seems better [now. Second turn was not so bad as the first. Now you have to land. Where is your instructor? Cut your motor and start your glide. Too steep. You pull the stick back, hoping that you will not stall. You seem to glide for hours. The ground comes up to meet you. You start to level off, hoping you don't run over your instructor. Where is he, anyway? The tail skid touches, wheels touch. Not three points, but not so bad for an amateur. You're some distance away from your instructor, who is sitting on his parachute in the middle of the field, watching. He motions you to take off again. This time you have more confidence and land nearer him. Solo schedule begins.

The month of "Dodo Days" drags on. What is this, a game? But the end is in sight. Election of class officers takes place. Recognition day. You speak to upper-classmen instead of saluting them and saying, "May I speak, sir?" What a relief that ceremony turned out to be!

The Cadet Dance. Dates—satisfaction and dissatisfaction. You've almost forgotten how to dance. Introduction—one or two strange looking females, colorful, if not esthetic. Pretty, some of them. Frantic signals, scouting parties, rescue work. Bed check. Ten demerits and two weeks' restriction to Post. Report to the O. D. hourly on open Post. You see, "it's an old cadet custom."

Holidays. Passes—week-end or for church? You must state *where* you are going. Mexico is forbidden. Rest? Maybe. Anyway, the glory of freedom and leisure for a little while. It seems so long. Won't Sunday evening ever come?

Back again. Take-offs, landings, eights on road, banks, and climbing turns, spins, forced landings and *headwork*. Twenty-hour check. More eliminations. Lost hopes, shattered ambitions. Deadly seriousness again. Who will be the next to go? Time seems to fly by. Things begin to seem more natural to you. More advanced work—chandelles, steep eights, barrels, 180's, 360's, loops and the thirty-five hour check nearly here. Your instructor working frantically on chandelles. Seems that you always fall off, skid or slip. It must stop. Name posted for check. Give up—know you can't pass, but you tried hard. FAILED, but you are to be rechecked later. You and your instructor work. You can now see that both must work in order for you to pass. Never thought of that before. Finally the day comes. Not so good, not so bad. You finish your check. Will it be go on, or go home? The check pilot says nothing. You wonder if you passed, even by a small margin. Minutes seem like hours. You summon up all your courage to ask him, but he speaks first, "On with your next phase work." You've passed! ! ! You feel you were lucky. You work harder.   Only twenty more hours and then the final check in the Primary course.   Gee, if that worrisome part of the course was only over!

Ground School.   No time to think about flying.   Early in the morning and late in the afternoons—just to fill up your time before and after flying.   Just another thing to keep you out of trouble.   Dry, hot—and can't they understand that you came here to learn to fly, that you attended schools and college before you came here. Motors, Navigation, Meteorology, Maps, Rigging and Busser.   Useful?   Yes, but so dry, especially when you want to fly and fly. Examinations. Re-examinations. Called in, bawled out.   Stay in at nights.   Study, study, is all they think you should do.

One more month and a new class of "dodos" will be here to go through the same bells, to go through the same tests and drills and inspections—to dream the same dreams—and to stand the same gaff.

The fifty-five hour check comes and goes.   Only two platoons in the corps now.   Formations, night flying, landing at a mark or in a circle, cross-wind take-offs and landing, and then the accuracy stage.   It's about over now.   The upper class visiting Kelly Field, looking over their new home, their new worries and work.

Graduating Day!   Reviews by both classes, speeches, congratulations and the final departure of the upper class.

New Flying Cadet officer appointed.   You are appointed the new Flying Cadet captain.   Why?   No one knows or cares.   New responsibilities in addition to your regular work.   Don't they understand that you are carrying all that you can carry? No—at least they don't seem to.

A week's rest before flying? "No." New cadets that you must show the new life to. You make the inspections, ring the bells. Drills, tours and gigs. You are saluted. You bawl out the new men. What do they think this is anyway? Such dumbjohns you have never seen before! Where did they get them—from the bushes? They will pass the food, pour the water. What are they here for anyway? They can't fly—a waste of time and money. You will be boss and give the commands. They will wear the "Green Tags." There goes one now. "On the double, Mister."

Flying starts again. You march down the road. Same Stage Commander, same instructor. New idea, this "follow through" system, in which the same instructor goes from the Primary Stage and PT's to "B" Stage and DH's and Basic Course.

New ships, larger and more powerful. How time does fly! Not like the old days. You wonder if the days seem as long for the new cadets as they were for you. A month goes by. Solo, without the old worry or the old thrill. Same type of work. Harder? Yes, but you know what it is all about now. You understand, you can see and think in the same line as your instructor without talking and without a whole lot of explanation.

Another recognition day. New class not so bad, but it was hard work. They finally saw daylight.

Another dance. Introducing the new cadets to the same girls —the "cadet girls"—that were introduced to you the same way.

The party is over. Same bed check, same scouting parties, same demerits, same tours. "Customs?"

Twenty-hour check coming up. But you are not worried now. You know what they want and you can do even more if they will let you. They don't know that on your solo flights you have tried out several new things. Not allowed—no, but you heard someone talk about it in the barracks, and why not if you are not caught? You are willing to take that chance. Full of confidence now—no more worry. Why do some of the lower-classmen look so bad? You guess why, but you didn't look that way when you were just starting. No?

Golf, tennis, volley ball, swimming and more parties. A date once in a while. Why hadn't you thought of this before? More leisure—mind is beginning to function a little more normally again.

More ground school. New subjects—not so hard. You have the swing of the thing now. Buzzer and still more buzzer—the only thing you dislike.

Reveille, drills, inspections and bed check still. Stay out once in a while. Stuff beds—caught and an eight-mile hike. Good exercise except for the tired feeling, sore back and blistered feet. Will wait for a while before taking another chance.

Flying? Yes, still flying, but it's different now. No more worries except for the thirty-five hour check. Just like the old checks—not bad, not good. Loud talking, bawling out. Stay in at night. More rest is needed. The check pilot said "Slump." What is it? No one knows. What causes it? No one knows. Got it? Yes. New instructor. Take-off for the week-end.

See new scenery, new things. Come back feeling great. Begin to improve. Have to be careful now. Too close to the end of the race to stop now. Last phase check—what you expected. Things are easy now. You feel like flying. Make your eights around pylons, slip it into land. Just all in a day's work. Passed, of course. Ready for final check.

Another table taken out of the mess hall.

Ground School is over ? ? ? ? ?

Final check. Report to Flying Office. Lie around all day. Couldn't get to you today. Report back next day. You report back next day. Final Test Pilot comes out; calls your name; tells you what to do. Main thing is to *fly*. You climb into the ship. It has a number and two zeros on it. Yes, that was the ship that caused more grief. Yet, it caused more happiness too than any other ship on the field. Easy to fly. Rigged, was it? Pleasure to fly it. Landed O. K. Back for formation and night flying. Not so bad. You have done the same things in the old PT's.

Cross-country trips. Where are you, anyway? Why did the clouds have to come in. You wish you had studied navigation a little harder. Land to ask a farmer. Yes, you are all right. You were good on forced landings. Proceed to place designated. The instructor didn't ask you why you were late. So you said nothing.

Practice for review for graduation.

Graduation day. Pass in review. Not so bad. You stayed in place and made your last landing at the *Primary Flying School*. Same speeches, same congratulations. Turning in beds, trunks.

Packing up. Last dinner, and on the way to Kelly Field for your last four months of training. As you pass down the road you notice new men in civilian clothes reporting in. Would they go through the same worry, grief and apprehension? How you pity them, yet envy them.

Kelly Field, or the Advanced Flying School. You have seen it every day or have heard it every day for the last eight months. But this time it is different. You are there. New barracks, new beds, new bells. No more worries. New life, new ships and new types.

Flying starts with transition. Who will ever forget the famous family of 02's? The "A," "B," "C," and the "H." You practice landings, formations and everything they had taught you at the Primary School. You had to be proficient on each ship, each type. They all flew alike but each had its own peculiar characteristics.

Days fly by and you fly with them.

Specialization. You don't know what you want, so you finally select—

Pursuit. You fly AT4's and P-1's. Small and easy to handle —easy to barrel and dive. Such speed! You do every form of acrobatics, formation combat, balloon strafing. You even escort bombing ships on their mission to keep other planes from interfering with them. You are one of the fighters.

Attack. You fly A3's, a new ship with guns and bomb racks. You study geography with these ships. Altitude always zero. You rake the roads and trenches with your guns. You drop bombs on wagon trains and you hop hedges. You miss windmills, water tanks and chimneys. Night missions are just as easy as the others.

Observation. You fly 02's. Sweet ship! You become a lookout for the rest of the Army. Taught to see everything. Report accurately and forget nothing. Expert on radio. Buzzer now is useful. You call for the fire and report the hits and misses. You develop cat's eyes for night work. Dangerous, but very important.

Bombardment. You fly NB's and Keystones. You are the destructive gang. You drop big bombs that will destroy cities, forts or anything that they hit, and you make them hit what you want them to.   Large and heavy, but you enjoy them.

Ground School—Something new for you. Not the old subjects, but new ones pertaining to your work. You are now receiving training for real military work and nothing else. It is interesting. If you stay in the Army, you will want and need it.

Time is flying by. Have to buy new uniform, boots, Sam Browne belt, gold bars—and you have no money. Too many parties; too many dates—girls are to blame. How will you get them? Well, how did the rest do it? Telegrams—? Yes. You get them.

Gunnery, bombing, cross-countries, night cross-countries—all over.

Big maneuver and then return, and then graduation. You state whether you desire active service or intend to go back to civilian life and carry on in the commercial game.

Packing up, turning in all clothes. No, you will not need the

Blues any more. You are too happy now. Tomorrow! tomorrow!—and the end.

TOMORROW. Wake up at the same time, a little sad.
Stand your last reveille. Eat your last breakfast. No one seems
to want to talk. The BIG REVIEW and the LAST REVIEW
for lots of you. Back to the barracks. New uniforms, boots and
belts.

Speeches.

Congratulations.

WINGS! ! !

A few good-byes, a few handshakes. Off to catch the train—
to carry some back to their homes—old friends, old loves; others
to their new stations to active duty.

Yes, there was lots of worry—grief—apprehension.

But—WINGS! ! ! !

LEARNING TO FLY COMMERCIALLY

BY ARO E. MAHARG

AVIATION had lain dormant, with hardly any perceptible impetus until Colonel Charles A. Lindbergh completed his epochal flight to Paris. The world was left gasping with the audacity of this seemingly impossible feat. The population of two continents, thrilled at the future of aviation, became "air-minded" overnight. No amount of aviation publicity, deeds or spectacular events accomplished what, in the space of 36 hours, Lindbergh did. Tremendous strides in every aviation line were made within a very few months. Aviation became the "dream Mecca" of countless thousands of the world's younger population, not to mention the many enthusiasts who were well along in years. Institutions of learning inaugurated various courses pertaining to aviation. Even high schools and grade schools, however remote from the hub of civilization, had their aviation courses within a short period of time. Aviation, through the medium of the many numerous aviation magazines and papers, reached into the innermost depths of the country. The youth of the country became fired with enthusiasm and the desire to emulate Lindbergh within the shortest possible time. The blasé city dweller was no less enthused. What enthusiasm! Everybody from the bootblack to the bank president wanted to become a "pilot."

Hundreds of flying schools sprang up throughout the United States. Some were good. Some were bad and some were schools in name only. The majority fell under the latter category. An extensive advertising program was inaugurated. The main theme in their Opus was, "Let US Teach You to Fly." This was what the public had been waiting for. The demand for trained aviators was enormous according to their information. An initiatory course in flying was all that was necessary to permit one to step into a commercial position extending an astonishing financial remuneration.

And so these would-be aerial argonauts dashed off to the nearest aviation school with a limited amount of "coin of the realm," which, in the majority of cases, did not exceed $300.00 and in most cases represented their savings for considerable time. They expected to become full-fledged pilots with aerial experience of from twenty to thirty hours. Had not the school promised them they would?

The illusion was soon shattered. Ten hours' dual training soon ate up this insignificant sum and the student was left "stranded." Here was an individual with ten hours' training, sufficient to enable him to distinguish ailerons from tail surfaces, when he had expected to become a mail pilot with the same amount of training. The result?—a bitter and disillusioned student. The inevitable happened. The student packed his helmet and goggles and returned home. Aviation had lost one sincere "booster."

While the public has become "air-minded" within a very short time, which to aviation is of the utmost importance, they also have been lax in realizing the extremely high cost of training. The consensus of public opinion seems to be that almost anyone can learn to fly with only a few hours' training. This is quite true, but with what degree of efficiency?

To become an aviator of sufficient skill to permit one to step into a position paying, say, $5,000.00 a year, entails the expenditure equal to the amount a college man spends during the course of his tuition. This, I know, sounds rather absurd but is an undisputable fact.

Too many schools are inclined to paint the path of aviation as an easy one and infer that the cost is very nominal. This is a serious drawback both to the student and the industry.

The average cost in the many schools that the writer has come in contact with is $30.00 per hour. A minimum of ten hours dual instruction and ten hours solo instruction is compulsory. At the completion of this training the student is supposed to be sufficiently skillful to pass the Department of Commerce tests for a Private Pilot's License. This license permits the holder only to fly an airplane for private use. It does not permit him to engage in commercial ventures; therefore, a very small income, if any, can be derived from this type of license. It is of no practical use except to a person owning his plane and this is a matter of considerable expense, far beyond the average student. The average cost of completing such a course is conservatively estimated as follows:

Living expenses while learning (approximately 8 weeks)
  $15.00 per week.................................$120.00
10 hours dual instruction at $30.00 per hour.......... 300.00
10 hours solo instruction at $30.00 per hour........... 300.00
Five hours additional solo time at $25.00 per hour...... 125.00
Helmet and goggles................................. 18.00
Flying suit 6.00
Lecture courses 20.00
Miscellaneous items, i.e., books, etc 25.00

                    $914.00

From the foregoing we see that the average cost of training for a Private Pilot's License is $914.00. This, you might say, is an initiatory course in flying and is a "white elephant" in so far as a commercial income is concerned.

The Limited Commercial License, which permits the holder to engage in limited commercial work, requires a minimum of fifteen hours dual and thirty-five hours solo flying time, analyzed as follows:

15 hours dual instruction at $30.00 per hour...........$450.00
35 hours solo instruction at $25.00 per hour........... 875.00
Necessary flying equipment......................... 68.75
Living expenses—4 months at $60.00 per month....... 240.00

                    $1,633.75

This type of license permits the holder to engage in such aerial pursuits as dusting crops, flying freight and "hopping" passengers within a specified area designated by the Department of Commerce. It is extremely difficult for one who has completed 50 hours in the air to secure a position due to the many pilots with much more air time who are at present unemployed. The only way to secure these much needed hours is either purchase your own plane, which, in the majority of cases is inadvisable unless the purchaser has unlimited means, or rent a plane at the usual rate of $25.00 per hour. In the event that the latter course is pursued, a tremendous item of expense is incurred.

The goal of all aviators is the Department of Commerce Transport Pilot's License. Possessing this license, the holder can engage in almost any commercial venture. Two hundred air hours are required before this license is granted and a very thorough practical and theoretical examination is given the applicant. The cost of training for such a license varies from $4,500.00 to $5,500.00 and extends over a period of three years. Do not these figures equal almost those of a college education?

A wonderful help, both to the industry and student, would be the impressing upon the student, by the school to which he applies for flight training, the enormous cost and the uncertainty of commercial positions at the expiration of their courses. No doubt this would deter a great many students from taking flying training, but in the end it would be a great benefit to all concerned.

The aviation enthusiast with a limited amount of capital, imbued with the desire to fly, merits the same advice as given to stock market devotees: "Stay out unless you have the cash."

THE AIR PATROL OF THE COAST GUARD

BY A. G. WEST

WHEN the United States Government first established the air patrol, which for some years past has watched over and protected a part of the most dangerous section of our North Atlantic seaboard, it is probable that no one realized that this nation was to be a pioneer in thus organizing an efficient system of.life-saving by aircraft.

And just as the Forest Service not so long before had blazed a new trail through the dim aisles of age-old forests toward science and knowledge of saving trees by woodcraft, so the Aviation Unit of the U. S. Coast Guard blazed an air trail of safety for mariners and for the freighted "Purple Argosies" of the commerce of a nation.

Perhaps it may seem curious that it was not at once appreciated to what an extent this new system of scouring the seas along our far-flung coast line might mean in terms of security for lives and property. Aviation had made tremendous strides during the war, and, as a result, there had come something of an adjustment toward this new mode of transportation, and a renaissance of interest as to its future in business and trade. But it is more than likely that this same interest was, in many cases, little more than a frugal gesture to utilize the trained pilots and surplus planes of war days, and to adapt them, as well as might be, to the needs of a busy and fast-growing nation.

These needs were particularly acute with respect to the fishing industry, whose financial gain or loss is so greatly dependent upon the vagaries of the weather, and whose bases of operations must shift with the season in spite of gales that might ravage the coast. The thought thus came that with the aid of airplanes, more men and their dories might be located and picked up after storms, and more contraband might be detected, than with the older and slower method of combing that same area with the patrol boats. Or that perhaps a combination of the two methods might be the most effective of all.

And so it proved. But as in many another instance where the use of aircraft has been in question and where the deeply-rooted traditions of the sea have been involved, selling this idea to the officials was by no means easy, and the start of the air patrol was, in consequence, so modest as to have discouraged a less ardent band of enthusiasts.

In the first place, there was no hangar. But that was soon remedied by borrowing a tent hangar from the Army Air Corps. The new unit had no plane either, and, what was worse, no money with which to buy one. The Navy was sufficiently interested in the venture to loan the Coast Guard a new plane, if assurance were given that it would be well cared for.

At Squantum, Mass., there is a large and hospitable naval air station. It is there that many of the college youths of New England have taken their flight training for the Naval Reserve

each summer.   With the aid and encouragement of this organization, the Coast Guard Aviation Unit collected itself together.

The excitement was intense when the crates arrived with the
new seaplane, which proved to have an excellent engine, and
fortunately so. Although history fails to have recorded a
christening, the U. S. Coast Guard Aviation Patrol took off
shortly after the new ship had been uncrated and assembled,
with the pilot, Lieut. Leonard Melka, at the stick for the test
flight.

It had been quite a problem where to select the site for the
base, which was nothing more than a bunch of rock lying off
Gloucester, and known as Ten Pound Island.   Pilots flew over
there from Squantum, and shook their heads gloomily.   They
returned with sound advice, of which the gist ran somewhat as
follows: "You're crazy.   That place is full of rocks and boulders.
How do you think you are going to get in and out of there with a
plane?"   But the work went right ahead, rocks or no rocks,
and long after dark and up until midnight the pilot and his
assistant carved out the base from this eyrie.

The patrol began with two flights a day up and down the
coast of Massachusetts and Maine.   The mechanic was a
fortunate choice; he had been grabbed off a patrol boat for this
particular labor after a study had been made of the best motor
machinists in the fleet.   Inducting him into aviation was a
simple process, but before turning him loose in aeronautics, his
superior officers firmly impressed him with the fact that, if the
engine failed at any time, it was extremely likely that he would
be among those present in the plane at the moment it was forced

down. There was also the factor of flight pay, and this item, together with the fact that the men in aviation have a chance to be with their families, was an added incentive for him to be extraordinarily careful in his work, for in the Coast Guard no man is so valuable that he cannot be immediately replaced. With the first bit of careless work, each member of the unit realizes that he stands a strong chance of being re-transferred to one of the patrol boats at sea.

The net result of this scheme, by the way, is so effective that the Coast Guard is said to have had but *one* forced landing and no crashes in all its history in aviation.   In view of the fact that it has flown hundreds of thousands of square miles during a period covering in all about twelve years, over foggy and dangerous seas, in all kinds of wind and weather, this is something of a record.

The new form of aerial protection by the plane found instant favor with the wives and families of the men of the fishing fleet off Gloucester. The pilot made a patrol before and after every storm, and men who had been reported lost or missing were located and word sent to the nearest patrol boat to pick them up.

Much valuable gear is often lost after storms from the fishing boats, and these have been reported by the pilot, and thus recovered. Men bucking the seas in open boats have been aided before a tragedy occurred. On one occasion a woman called up the base during a storm and said that she had a friend whose husband was overdue four days. She wanted to know what the Coast Guard could do toward finding him. There was a stiff wind blowing at the time, but the woman was so insistent that the commander finally felt that something could be done in spite of the fact that it was too rough to send a patrol boat out. Consequently, a plane was sent out for the search. The pilot took off in what he admits was a "pretty good breeze" and shoved on up the coast to see what he could find of this missing husband. He scoured the seas all along the way, as far as Portland•Lightship, and zigzagged back into various harbors and inlets to see if the boat was laid up anywhere. When he flew into Biddeford Harbor, there was the boat, safe and sound. Its occupants were waiting for the storm to subside . . . and the word was soon relayed by this aerial envoy.

All that area gets a good deal of the bad weather that drifts in from the Tail of the Banks, off Labrador, which is notoriously foggy. And if this is bad for small boats, it is equally dangerous for airplanes. On one occasion, Lieutenant Melka was out on his patrol when he ran into fog. When he wanted to land, he found he couldn't see to do so, though he thought he was near the base. He radioed to his chief, "Where are we?"

Commander Van Paulsen radioed back, "We can hear your motor right overhead. Better try up north and see how it is!"

Melka headed north, but it was just as bad there. He then came back and determined to stick right around there if it took him all morning. After a time, he received a radio from the base, "Fog slightly lighter," and he continued to fly back and forth at around 2,500 feet as he waited impatiently for the fog to lift.

Finally he received another message from Van Paulsen, saying, "Visibility a quarter of a mile." With this cheering news, he decided to try to descend if he could locate a small patch that was any brighter. He managed to come in and land her right near the breakwater. But had he been far out at sea, or without a radio, there might have been a different conclusion to the flight.

During the time that the two famous French aviators, Coli and Nungessor, were due to reach America from their transatlantic flight, both Commander Van Paulsen and Lieutenant Melka were flying in search of them in the midst of sleet, snow and storm. It was "snowing to beat the band" as the pilot put it, but these two Coast Guard fliers went out 200 miles at sea in their effort to find the missing men.

Soon after the organization of this unit, its value in locating rum ships was recognized as well worth any effort to keep the outfit going. The rum runners had formed the comfortable habit of having their ships lie offshore about 25 miles, where they were unloaded at their ease by small fast boats. Lieutenant Melka had discovered some eighteen or twenty of these ships on one of his earliest flights. Since there was no radio in the plane in those days, he recorded the names of the ships, turned back to the base, which radioed to the nearest cutter to attend to the "rummies."

Almost immediately, the Coast Guard officials began to realize what an asset that plane was going to be. Nor was their confidence misplaced, for according to the records of the aviation unit, some 75 per cent of the rum ships captured have been first located from the air.

The pilot was daily warned, cautioned and exhorted by his commander not to fly out more than twenty miles to sea, for there was no relief plane to go out for him in case of a forced landing. But as time passed, and the rum ship captains became more and more nervous about anchoring inside the 20-mile limit, Lieutenant Melka had a hunch that by flying out about twice as far, he would find twice as many rum ships. Moreover, he knew of a little shoal spot about 75 miles off a certain ledge. On the next fine day, he headed toward this rendezvous, and was gratified to find that his hunch was absolutely correct. In fact, there was a very large ship there, with cases and cases of liquor piled high on her decks and no effort at concealment at all.

At about that time, it was the practice of the pilot to fly over the cutters, and having flagged the captain and signaled that he had a message to deliver, pass down the message carrier. Captain Wheeler, in command of a cutter on duty in that section, became used to co-operating with the plane in this way, and as soon as it appeared, had a boat trailing astern of the ship to catch the message in. This was contained in a small square of cork, sewed in canvas and painted brightly in yellow. A hollow space was made and the note put in and corked up, and since it was light in weight, was not apt to injure anyone in falling. When the captain had received the message, he blew a blast or two on his steam whistle, and though Melka could not hear it, he counted the puffs of steam coming out for his answer.

One day, Captain Wheeler said he wanted to go up for a flight so that he could see some of the things they had told him about the game the speed boats were playing. The pilot took the plane up and throttled down so they could watch three speed boats try to draw the patrol boats away from a rum ship. The

Coast Guard Sea and Air Patrol
Off the New England Shore

first act of this little comedy showed the decoy speed boat come up on the horizon from seaward as though it intended to come inshore. By passing off at a little distance, but well in sight of the patrol boats, he naturally gave them the impression that he was trying to conceal the fact that he had a cargo of liquor and hoped to make a run with it. One of the patrol boats at once gave chase. The speed boat had no cargo, of course, and by opening up its engine only enough to make it interesting, managed to egg the patrol boat into pursuit.

At about this time, a second speed boat came up on the horizon at another angle. This second boat came along fairly near to the boat on patrol and with no big ship in sight to watch, the Government boat gave chase. Men on board a third speed boat, lying by with a full crew at about ten minutes' distance, were watching this scene through high-powered binoculars, and when it was evident that both patrol boats were busily engaged with the two decoy speed boats in the other direction, so that the road to the rum ship was clear, rushed madly up to it. Only about five minutes were required to throw the bags of wine and cargo nets, and perhaps ten minutes in all was enough to turn the trick for the enterprising rum runner. The speed boat then turned toward shore, having dumped stores and messages on the "rummy" during the exchange.

While all this was going on, the decoy boats had slowed down, and had permitted the Government patrol to overtake and board them. But all this took time, and precious time, too. There was, of course, no contraband on the two decoy boats, and the patrol's efforts were wasted.

It was all very interesting to watch, and the captain of the cutter especially enjoyed it as the plane crept up on the speed boats and took in the fine points of this illegal maneuver. Thus was the air patrol able to observe the methods employed by rum runners. All the boats on patrol were warned of this little game, and, in time, this was one of the things that broke up the famous "Rum Row."

Several years after the Coast Guard had initiated its aviation service, and inasmuch as it had proved so notable a success, Congress passed legislation providing for ten air stations which were to be maintained in the same way as the original one. Unfortunately, this generous gesture amounted to very little, for the funds to apply to these air stations were conspicuously lacking and have remained lacking ever since.

Enough was granted, however, to do something toward making a start at an aviation unit at Moorhead City, off the coast of Carolina. This section about Cape Hatteras has long been known to mariners as the "Graveyard of the Atlantic," for it has had more than its share of tragic wrecks. This base was gradually forced into the sea by the loss of land, and was later abandoned, though the unit at Base 9, at Cape May, has done splendid work from the hangars owned by the Navy.

The latter is also a very dangerous section. In the spring, it is regularly visited by the Gloucester fishing fleet because of the mackerel found off the Jersey coast at that time. Lieut. Walter Anderson and Chief Gunner Thrunn have shared the patrols there for several years, and have a fine group of enlisted men in their unit to back up their flying. It must always be remembered that it is largely the character of work done by the mechanics that tells the story in aviation. Piloting the plane is only part of the job.

A base was started in southern waters last year, near Fort Lauderdale. The flying there has become extremely important, since there is so much activity in and near the water with various regattas and outboard motor races. The dramatic rescue of these small speed boats at the regattas is one of the most interesting of the many ways in which the air unit operates on patrol. For example, in one race between Boston and New York, planes followed the entire course of the race. A Senior Officer was in charge of the patrol, and the two planes on duty reported continually to him by wireless, so that he was informed at all times of the progress of the race itself, as well as of the accidents which seem inevitable on such occasions. Five of these speedy little crafts capsized on this particular day, and the news was in each case radioed by the flier overhead to the nearest patrol boat on duty. The boat then rushed to the rescue and picked up the men.

Another interesting example of the use of radio from these planes is the immediate report from the pilot who has sighted a school of fish. The radio message is at once relayed from the base to the Master Mariners' Association, where it is turned over to the nearest radio broadcast station, which announces it over the air.

Practically all of the fishing boats at Gloucester are equipped with radio receiving sets, and one or two with modern transmitters. Thus the news of the school is immediately available to the fleet, and, according to Lieutenant Melka, the first boats often set out toward the location reported within fifteen or twenty minutes of the time the news is radioed to the base.

The Coast Guard flying usually must be carried on at a low altitude. Generally speaking, the patrol is flown at an altitude of 500 or 750 feet. The occupants of the plane wear no parachutes, since of course their route is over water. There is, however, a kapok pillow that if needed is supposed to act as a sort of life preserver. In addition, as in Navy planes, there are extra supplies, including chocolate and malted milk tablets, hard-tack, bait, fishing lines and fish hooks, Coston signals (green and red), canteens of water, and spare parts for the plane in small kits, etc.

With the tremendous increase of air traffic in America, there will soon be greater use of the coastwise air routes. Hand in hand with this need, the Coast Guard plans an expansion that shall stand ready to serve these aerial travelers.

Within the past few months, a new system of protection for coastwise air traffic has been devised by Lieut. Commander Norman Hall in charge of the Aviation Unit of the Coast Guard. This is now in active service. All planes flying past Coast Guard stations are carefully checked from one to the other, after notification is received from the airport that the plane has taken off. Planes so reported that fail to turn up within a reasonable length of time are reported to the authorities selected by the airport, or the owners of the plane. If the plane is two hours overdue, a search is started immediately under the direction of the District Commander. In this way, aid is almost immediately available to the pilot in distress; he is not left for days untended if forced down on a lonely shore far from aid.

The U. S. Coast Guard has been fortunate in having brought together a small and hardy group of what are probably the most enthusiastic fliers in the world. They seem to thrive on an indifference that would have stifled any other service, for when millions were appropriated by Congress for other purposes, these men had to cling like a barnacle to their old and outworn planes. They seemed to have enjoyed flying under conditions that ordinarily would bring back the average pilot to the safety of his hangar. Fog, snow and sleet are all part of the day's work, just as they are to the air mail pilot.

The prestige of the life-saving unit of the nation has been greatly enhanced by this band of some five or six pilots and their loyal group of motor machinists who service the planes. But it is work that has been done simply, quietly and without ostentation. It is only the men who go down to the sea in ships, who have been caught in small boats in storms, who can truly tell the story of the Aviation Unit of the Coast Guard.

COMMERCIAL AVIATION IN THE YUKON

BY R. N. MILLER

FLYING an American open-cockpit plane in temperatures frequently forty below, over rough, uninhabited country in which a forced landing spells slow, painful death, two young Yankee pilots are making air travel a commonplace in the sub-arctic Yukon territory of Canada.

Clyde G. Wann, late of Arkansas, and John M. Patterson, late of Colorado, operations manager and chief pilot, respectively, for the Yukon Airways and Exploration Company, Ltd., have maintained a fairly regular air mail and passenger service (even in dead winter) between their base at Whitehorse and Dawson, four hundred miles away. Four hours is usually required to fly over the desolate stretch, whereas a caterpillar tractor requires 12 to 14 days between towns, and a dog team even more.

Last fall Wann and Patterson flew the first commercial airplane (a Whirlwind-powered Eaglerock) to reach the rugged vicinity of Whitehorse from the United States under its own power. Wann has written a detailed account of the flight and a description of the Yukon company's novel methods of combatting the frigid winter climate.

216

A significant feature of the 4,000-mile flight is that the Eagle-rock paid for itself on its way to Whitehorse.   En route up the Pacific Coast, the pair stopped at every likely town.   At many the natives had never seen an airplane.   The entire population of some centers turned out to inspect the plane, and a rushing passenger business followed.   According to Wann, his passenger receipts from the time he left Vancouver, B. C., until his arrival at Whitehorse, amounted to $6,700, or slightly more than the cost of the plane.   The ship stood up admirably under the severe trip, in which it flew 18,000 miles, carried 1,500 passengers, and made over 800 landings.

Flying up the coast, Patterson and Wann frequently were forced to wire ahead for information on the available landing fields.   At Prince George, Hazelton and Whitehorse they used fields prepared for the New York-to-Nome fliers in 1920.   At Hazelton the pair graded a 1,700-foot runway before attempting to take off with a heavy load of gasoline and supplies.   At other towns the airmen used grain and hay fields, measured and marked according to their telegraphic orders.

The longest hop, from Hazelton to Telegraph Creek, carried the pair over 320 miles of some of the most rugged country in North America.   Since no accurate maps of the territory were available, they navigated by the hit-or-miss landmark method. It was six degrees below zero when they finally landed at Tele-graph Creek.

The fliers left Colorado Springs early in September while the National Air Races were still in progress at Los Angeles.   Land-ing at Salt Lake City on the first morning out, they were surprised to find a large welcoming committee swarm around and extend the joyful hand. The large letters on the plane required on all Canadian craft had led the crowd to mistake them for one of the Canada-to-California racers due that day at the Utah capital.

After leaving Vancouver, they flew passengers at Chilliwack, Kamloops, Vernon, Kelowna, Penticton, Williams Lake, Quesnel, Prince George, Vanderhoof, Burns Lake, Smithers, Hazelton, Telegraph Creek, Atlin and Carcross.

The entire trip was free from mishaps with the exception of two broken wheels, caused when Pilot Patterson was forced to ground-loop on landing in a small, rough field.

Operating aircraft in the sub-arctic regions is not as tough as might be imagined, according to Wann. He has flown the company's Eaglerock at temperatures as low as 42 below, without discomfort to pilot or passengers. Heavy flying suits, face masks and fur-lined helmets break the frigid propeller blast.

Until it can build a big one, the young company is depending on small "motor hangars." Each night the plane is drawn up to a small building near the headquarters, sheltering no more than the motor. A canvas fits snugly around the cowling behind the motor, and a hot-air pipe is extended from the jacket around the stove to a point under the carbureter. On extremely cold days, a blow torch is used to force hot air through the pipe. Heated air warms the gas, and the motor starts easily. It is closely cowled in to a point just below the spark plugs. Oil lines are wrapped with asbestos wicking, shellacked and taped.

The oil tank is covered with asbestos and even the cowling louvres are covered.

At first, when the pilot throttled down to land, his motor cooled so fast that not infrequently it cut out completely. Special carbureter cowling remedied this trouble.

Barnstorming continues to be one of the company's chief sources of revenue. The inhabitants are hardy souls who enjoy flying and usually are able to pay for long rides. One Sunday afternoon recently at Penticton, trade grew so rushing that Pat made eleven "ten-minute" hops in one hour. The crowd had its enthusiasm up, and as Wann explains, "We tried not to keep them waiting longer than necessary."

The company has contracted to fly a number of trappers and prospectors to isolated spots in the rich, unexplored Mayo-Keno district. The Eaglerock will land them on a lake in the heart of the region, fully equipped for a summer's expedition. The adventurers ordinarily would mush throughout a greater part of the season before reaching their scene of operations.

Few places in the world are so well suited for aerial development as the northern part of Canada, Wann declares. The few planes in the country are awakening the populace to the fact. Despite the relatively small population and long distances between towns, there is not a corresponding lack of money nor interest in aviation. The thousands of lakes make first rate landing fields in both winter and summer.

For a great many years vast areas in the northern part of our continent have remained comparatively unproductive, mainly because of the difficulties in reaching isolated regions of virgin wealth.　Throughout Canada and in Alaska, aviation is rapidly overcoming those natural barriers which have blocked man's penetration into the north country.　Here the business of flying is finding another field of important usefulness.

Because of their inaccessibility, many thousands of square miles remain untrapped, unexplored and unprospected.　Airplanes alone can make this isolated territory productive of its great untouched wealth in furs and minerals.

ARMY FLIGHT TRAINING

*The History and Present Status of Army Flight Training is
Given Here in Graphic Vein*

BY MAJOR GENERAL JAMES E. FECHET
Chief of the Air Corps

IT is now twelve years since the Army has gone into the intensive training of flyers. The entry of this country into the World War had the effect of causing this engrossing activity to spring up overnight. The Allies demanded airplanes and pilots and it was simply up to America to supply this demand despite the fact that it was hardly prepared to do so.

The outbreak of the war found the Aviation Section of the Signal Corps with a commissioned personnel of but 65 officers. Among this mere handful of men were some very skillful pilots, but the exigencies of the period demanded that they be placed in executive and key positions in this country as well as overseas. It was clearly out of the question to utilize any of them in the capacity of flying instructors. And so in the first few months of the war the aviation branch of the Army was forced to rely almost entirely upon civilian flying instructors to train ambitious young men anxious to serve their country in a combatant branch of the military service which presented a particular appeal to them. How great this appeal proved to be may be deduced from the fact that by the time the Armistice was signed the aviation branch of the Army had grown to such pro-

221

portions that its commissioned and enlisted personnel consti-
tuted an organization exceeding the pre-war strength of the
entire Army.

The dearth of flying instructors at the beginning and for several months subsequent to the outbreak of the war was gradually overcome as students graduated from the various flying
schools, which had been established throughout the country,
and those graduates evincing adaptability as flying instructors
were assigned on such duty. Students who received training
in this country during the war were only taught to fly the training type of ship, the old Curtiss "Jenny"; those who were sent
overseas with the ultimate object of engaging the enemy on the
front lines attended advanced flying schools or instruction centers
in France, Italy and England and were taught to fly pursuit,
bombardment or observation planes before they were assigned
to combatant squadrons.

At the cessation of hostilities the United States was faced with
the unusual situation of possessing a superabundance of young
aviators, many of them highly trained and skillful military pilots.
To retain them on active duty was out of the question, since no
provision had been made for the Air Service as a permanent
combatant branch of the Army. It was also foreseen that, even
were provision made by Congress for a separate aviation branch,
its peace-time strength would be but a fraction of its expanded
war-time strength. The natural result was that honorable dis-
charges from the Army were carried out by the wholesale until
what may be termed a skeleton organization remained. When
Congress in 1920 passed an amendment to the National Defense

Act, creating the Air Corps as a combatant branch of the Army, examinations were held in the summer of that year of those men who professed a desire to be permanently commissioned therein. Even at this late date, however, the commissioned personnel of the Air Corps does not measure up to the authorized strength.

Despite the continuous discharge of commissioned flying personnel, as well as enlisted men, from the time of the signing of the Armistice until the close of the year 1920, flying training activities were carried on, although on a greatly reduced scale. It was foreseen that, in the event of another war emergency, the same old story would be re-enacted of utilizing the Regular Army merely as a nucleus for the expanded war strength Army to follow. The World War furnished a bitter lesson, and the War Department was fully determined to profit thereby.

In November, 1918, America was fully prepared for war, with the machinery well oiled to send a constant stream of trained flyers overseas. With the Dove of Peace again hovering overhead, however, it was realized that the large majority of the war-time flyers, going back to civil occupations, would in a few years lose touch with the flying game and their usefulness to the country would dwindle as the years went on. War-time emergency officers who were discharged from the Army were given commissions in the Reserve Corps, but the Air Corps Reserve presented a somewhat different problem than the other branches of the Army. Flying is essentially a young man's game, and to be proficient in the art constant practice is necessary. The practice of Reserve flyers going to the comparatively few flying fields which remain in operation in order to obtain flying practice was encouraged, but it was appreciated that only a small percentage of them would be able to avail themselves of the opportunity. The battle of life is a paramount issue, and very few men in the business or professional world can afford to divert even part of their valuable time to keep themselves fit for military duty.

It was with these considerations in mind that the Air Corps continued to operate several flying schools and encouraged applications from qualified young men for appointment as Flying Cadets, their reward upon graduation being a commission in the Air Reserve. It was felt that a constant flow of trained young flyers into the Reserve would prove a great boon to the country in time of need.

For a few years following the close of the war, primary flying schools were maintained at Carlstrom Field, Arcadia, Fla., and March Field, Riverside, Calif., with Advanced Flying Schools at Post Field, Fort Sill, Oklahoma, and Kelly Field, San Antonio, Texas. The necessity for further economy in the administration of the Army tended towards a continuance of demobilization measures, with the result that the effects thereof were felt in flying training carried on by the Army to the extent that the schools at Post and March Fields were closed. It was decided to concentrate flying training activities at San Antonio, Texas, and this led to the abandonment of Carlstrom Field and the removal of the Primary Flying School to Brooks Field. Kelly Field was designated as the school for all advanced flying training. These two schools are still in operation, as is also March Field, which was re-established as a Primary Flying School in the latter part of 1927 following the passage by Congress of the Air Corps five-year expansion program.

The year 1927 was a notable one in the history of American aviation, the many outstanding aeronautical achievements that year, among them the transatlantic flights of Lindbergh, Chamberlin and Byrd, the Hawaiian flights of Lieuts. Maitland and Hegenberger and others, causing an unprecedented interest in aviation. Both military and commercial aviation benefited by this revival of interest. One needs but pick up a current issue of some of the prominent aeronautical magazines and compare same with issues published in 1926 to appreciate the great change which the aeronautical industry has undergone in the short space of two years.

The growing air-mindedness of the American public caused its influence to be felt in the Army Air Corps in more ways than one, but since the subject I am dealing with is flying training, it is significant to remark that the Air Corps at the present time is able to approve only a fraction of the vast number of applications from young men all over the country who desire to obtain flying training at the Air Corps schools. This sudden wealth in applications for cadet appointments has enabled the Air Corps to change its policy with respect to the acceptance of same and to exercise much greater discrimination in the selection of candidates deemed qualified for such appointment.

Insufficient accommodations at the two Air Corps Primary Flying Schools rendered it necessary to limit new classes at both of them to about 110 students each. New classes are entered every four months—March 1st, July 1st and November 1st, which means that, with graduation classes of 100%, over 600 students would graduate from the Primary Schools each year. However, only about sixty per cent of those students who start the course are able to keep up the pace during the eight months' grind, and so by the time the Primary School graduates pass through the additional four months of intensive training at the Advanced Flying School at Kelly Field, approximately half the number of those who started flying training receive their "wings."

There is no such possibility as merely slipping through the Army flying schools. When a student graduates from the Advanced School, he is an aviator in every sense of the word. There is no element of doubt as to a graduate's ability to pilot a military airplane. During a student's career at the Army flying school he is always under the close scrutiny of his instructors. If any weaknesses crop out in his flying, he is checked up by several instructors and, if he evidences inability to correct his faults, he is eliminated from further instruction. "Natural aptitude" is a byword at the Army flying schools, and lack of it has dealt disappointment to many an aspirant for the much coveted "wings" of the Army.

The Air Corps does not believe in taking chances. It holds that human life is very dear to everyone and that it is folly to permit a student to continue his training when it just isn't in him to become a military flyer.

The flying training system used by the Army is about as thorough as human brains have been able thus far to contrive. The system is the result of many years of painstaking and constant development. Today it stands as a model system, known the

*Take-off and Review, Primary Training
Class, Brooks Field*

world over, and patterned after by commercial flying schools now springing up in various sections of the country to fill the needs of commercial aviation.

The Air Corps has fully profited by past mistakes. There have been casualties in flying training in the early years of the flying schools, but these have been reduced until now a fatal accident in training is exceptionally rare. With gradual improvement in instruction methods and the procurement of new and up-to-date training ships, it is but natural to expect such progress.

WHERE DOES CONGRESS STAND?

BY HON. F. H. LA GUARDIA
Member of Congress

IF the United States has not a unified, well-equipped and the most efficient air service in the world, it is not the fault of Congress. It is the fault entirely of the Army and Navy. Congress is now air-minded. It is in the mood to provide money generously for the development of aviation.

Naturally in aviation legislation, as well as appropriation, Congress is guided entirely by the advice of so-called experts. Aviation, so far as its relation to Congress is concerned, has to date been mostly from the military side. Congress up to 1914 had little confidence in the development, practicability, and future of aviation. A few paltry dollars were appropriated for experimental purposes, but so little encouragement was given by Congress to aviation that, as everyone sorrowfully remembers, the Wright brothers were so discouraged that they took their plane to France where it seems there was a better understanding, more sympathy and perhaps more parliamentary vision.

After the World War in 1914, even Congress grew to learn that aviation was of the utmost importance for both offensive and defensive purposes. The growth, development and scope of aviation in the first three years of the World War was such as to make Congress feel very much ashamed of itself, owing to its neglect to keep abreast in this field. When 1917 rolled along and the United States entered the World War, Congress, in its anxiety to correct its sins of omission in the past, jumped at the opportunity to demonstrate its appreciation of aviation and appropriated six hundred and forty million dollars ($640,000,-000.00) for aviation. It was a lump sum appropriation. Congress practically said, "We have done nothing in the past. We have not experimented. We have no equipment. We have failed to appropriate heretofore. We know nothing about it. Here are six hundred and forty million dollars. Go ahead and build up an air service."

Out of the six hundred and forty million dollars the United States built up the finest personnel, flyers and enthusiasts in the whole world and collected an enormous amount of junk, obsolete equipment and cost-plus contracts. The flying personnel was the best, the equipment the worst, of any country in the world. Immediately after the signing of the Armistice the enthusiasm of the boys of the air service became contagious and there was a real movement in this country for the development of an air service. The cost-plus contractors and other junk dealers who had grown rich during the war were quick to grasp the situation and coined the catchy phrase, "We will never be caught unprepared again," and started their lobbies working in Washington.

Here was the plan. The Liberty motor, obsolete by the time it got into production, pieced together by well-meaning but mediocre engineers, and introduced to the country by the most efficient, active, expert group of publicity agents, was about all we had out of the six hundred and forty million dollars. We certainly had plenty of them. The "never to be caught unprepared again" plan consisted in getting Congress to appropriate for the manufacture (after the war) of twenty thousand additional Liberty motors, although we had over twelve thousand on hand then, and to put each motor in a can of oil and keep it in reserve for the next war. That sounds almost incredible now, but that proposition was actually suggested to the Military Affairs Committee of the Sixty-Sixth Congress.

By the time all the flyers got back from the other side and those who did not get across got back to their homes, the people of the country became better acquainted with the Liberty motor. The plan did not get very far. It was impossible for a time to estimate just how many of the motors we had on hand. I finally got a resolution through the House which required the War Department to submit a report to Congress showing the number of motors on hand. It is my recollection that the report showed that we had over twelve thousand Liberty motors on hand. It took me ten years to prevent the use of these old motors in new planes. It was not until the appropriation bill for the year 1929–1930, which passed the House last session of Congress, that I succeeded in writing into the bill a provision that these old motors must no longer be used in new planes. It took ten years of fighting, bickering, and loss of life and good planes to put an end to the use of these antiquated and obsolete motors.

This is but one instance showing the conservatism of the War Department, whose judgment Congress habitually follows. The air service, of course, is not to blame. But before the flyer or the engineer or the expert of the air service can get to Congress, he must go through so many channels, bureaus and offices, that by the time he reaches a Congressional Committee it is not the view of the air expert but that of the general staff who, as far as aviation is concerned, seems still to be fighting the Indian Wars over again.

When one gallant officer of the air service volunteered to talk and talk freely and to tell the truth, he was court-martialed. General William Mitchell did more for the good of aviation and for the education of Congress on this subject than all the rest of the country put together. The Army succeeded in court-martialing General Mitchell but it did not suppress him. The truth was out. Were it not for General Mitchell we would not have had the five-year air building program for Army and Naval aviation. Were it not for him Congress could never have learned to take the views of the general staff and the admirals with a grain of salt. Now if somebody else would only speak out again and get court-martialed perhaps Congress would entirely ignore the views of the general staff and the admirals, and establish a separate unified air service.

The unified air service is inevitable. It must come. Of course the general staff can retard it as it did the Lewis machine gun. Of course the Navy can hold to its own views for a certain length of time as it did in opposing the Ericcson propeller and the iron-clad ship. But not even the general staff or the Board of Admirals can stop progress. Just as General Mitchell shamed the country and brought about the first constructive building program, so will the progress of aviation and its development in other countries bring Congress to the point of disregarding the views based on purely selfish reason, coupled with lack of vision of the general staff and the Board of Admirals. A real honest-to-goodness separate, independent air service, headed by a civilian official of equal rank to the head of the Army and Navy, and administered and officered by flyers, is coming, and coming within a very short time.

Congress cannot be entirely blamed for the mistakes of the past. From now on, however, aviation has developed to such an extent and has demonstrated its possibilities and use so universally that if Congress continues to follow the views of the general staff and the admirals of the Navy, and continues separate services, it will be to blame and will be held responsible.

Personally, I do not believe that Congress will ever appropriate funds for another battleship; the airplane has made the battleship ineffective. This was definitely demonstrated at the bombing test in 1921 held in Hampton Roads. A few bombing planes, costing only a few thousand dollars, sent out on a war mission, can at will destroy the most perfect battleship on the sea, costing sixty million dollars. The only defense against an air offensive is aviation itself. To date no anti-aircraft gun has been developed to provide adequate defense. It makes good copy, and perhaps serves present purposes of the old generals, to stage an attack on New York every now and then with blank cartridges in the anti-aircraft guns and no bombs from the planes, and then report the large number of "theoretical hits." Planes today can fly over the range of the best anti-aircraft gun, and there can be no doubt in the mind of anyone, except the general staff and the battleship admirals, that any city today is vulnerable unless properly and adequately defended by an air force. As General Mitchell says, "A Navy as the determining element in sea warfare has lost its occupation." The Navy, however, certainly knows how to get its views across. It is great on publicity. In fact it has specialized in that subject. The Navy is a great advertiser. When it comes to lobbying, the railroads, oil, or the steel trust have nothing on the Navy.

Aviation has this advantage in the present stage of the art, in that each plane that flies can in the event of an emergency be quickly converted into a bomber or observation plane. A country which develops a large commercial aviation industry can in the event of an emergency become quickly prepared, notwithstanding the stubbornness of the general staff and Navy in times of peace.

Congress should do more to encourage and insist on the development of planes and motors. Experimental fields should be provided in every section of the country with available planes to try out any new motors, and motors to try out new types of planes. We should not permit the inventive genius of America to be entirely at the mercy of any group of men or group of companies, or at the mercy of Dayton or Philadelphia. The art is too young for that. Unless private industry develops proper and efficient flying schools at not unreasonable rates of tuition, the government should do more to train and develop pilots for commercial purposes. To date the Department of Commerce has done very good work. It has a tendency to become bureaucratic and this fault should be corrected before it becomes chronic.

Now is the time for all interested in aviation to come forward and express their opinion. Congress is in a receptive mood. I am hopeful for the future of aviation in this country. As to General Mitchell, to reverse Moran and Mack, I would say, "Even if he were not so good, I would still be with him."

20 FEET IN THE AIR

An Amusing Story of Cadet Days

BY LIEUT. THOMAS HUTCHINSON CHAPMAN

EARLY training has its sensations no less than those days of later flying. Possibly one remembers his first solo flights, because of their indelible imprint upon his memory, much better than events of his later and more experienced flying days. Seemingly, my early crashes and other peculiar happenings of the elementary training fields have stuck with me, while I have to refresh my memory on numerous occasions about happenings of the days after my commission and pilot designation finally arrived.

I became a member of one of the Navy's reserve "seaman second class for aviation training" classes by signing my name and telling my personal history and then asking three friends to endorse my application by attesting to my previous good character. Not all of the heroes were in uniform and I have always lauded the unselfish patriotism of these three friends. And their heroism was rewarded for, in a few days, I received a letter stating that "in accordance with your request, you are hereby assigned to duty under training, Royal Flying Corps School of Instruction, Toronto, Canada." I had enlisted for the reason that aviation had always appealed to me, and here was my chance to help out the great cause and at the same time follow my particular bent. And I was advised that "in accordance with my request." I felt somewhat like the young chap who, when asked why he didn't join the Army and fight, said that he could see no use in fighting because he wasn't mad at anybody.

I left for Toronto and without incident arrived and was immediately assigned to duty under instruction, which included nothing which I could see concerned actual flying. We spun and looped and gyrated around in utter abandon while in the classrooms and barracks, and all of us made our greatest flights and had our most serious crashes while safely seated in groups around on the parade ground. Soon we were admitted to the inner sanctum, where only those with "marked pilot material" entered. What we were to be marked with when we came out is another story, but we can skip over that lightly.

My career as a pilot began most inauspiciously under the direction of the Officer in Command, 85 Canadian Training Squadron, Royal Flying Corps. The Canadians adopted the policy of giving a student a minimum of instruction, since they repeatedly told us that a student could learn more in a crash, if he succeeded in getting out of it alive even though the ship was wrecked, than he could by piling up hours under instruction. Damages to ships were of little concern, if the student profited by it, and my own squadron, nicknamed the "Black Cat," had planes which were referred to as having only three lives left because they had been in six crashes already. It must be said that in the majority of first solos, the students who had a minimum of instruction invariably "got away with it" safely.

Most of us were turned loose at about three hours and a half, but not for long. We usually nosed over or made some such characteristic of the young fledgling landing, and went under instruction again. We were sent off mainly to get the feel of the air, and some of us got not only that, but the feel of the ground as well. So we passed on to the qualified stage and began to mount up our hours so that we could transfer our activities to the advanced training squadrons.

Some three such hours had passed when I asked permission one morning to make a short cross-country to the neighboring airdrome about fifteen miles away. In line with the Canadian policy of allowing the student any privilege whatever, so long as it appeared to be helping him to become independent in his piloting, I was granted permission. I started out in one of the good old Dep control Jennies. I was not thoroughly acquainted with the ship or the air and while I reached my destination without incident, I began to wonder as soon as I was safely on the ground just how I would get back. I suppose the young runaway has the same thoughts after he has made his first sortie.

Some of my buddies of the classroom days were stationed at this airdrome and and I soon forgot my worries about the return trip. It was apparent, however, that I must make the start, for it was rapidly approaching the zero hour for tea. The British are insistent that ships be returned at the time indicated on departure, and while I would have preferred this

time to remain for tea, I decided that it would be the better
part of valor to remain in the good graces of the officers of my
home squadron. So amid many good wishes, I took off for
the return trip. I had only been in the air a short time when
it was evident that the motor was a bit worried about my
return and began to whimper in sympathy. And in addition
it began to look like rain. But it was merely a case of "Giddap,
there, Napoleon," and on we went, fretfully. I tried to stifle the
sobs and incoherent sputterings by manipulating the throttle,
thinking the gas line might be clogged. I was not to be successful, for the intermittent outbursts from the sick cylinders
kept up, but spurred with a desire to stay up as long as the old
crate would let me, I plowed on. Now I was hindered by an
assemblage of antagonistic winds. I could not climb and I
could not land, or at least I failed to see how I could get down
in the mass of brush and trees with any degree of dignity or
safety. I had previously had similar trouble during one of
my flights with an instructor and I had a horror of again being
set down in a clump of unfriendly trees.

Fortunately there was just enough power to keep me in the
air at about three hundred feet. The rough air persisted and
I could not help but think of the poor colored man admiring the
airplane at the carnival. The manager approached and implored
the colored man to fly the ship because his regular pilot was sick.
"You won't be hurt or anything like that, Henry, because I
know the man that made this airplane." "Well," said Henry,
after scratching his head a moment, "you might know the man
what made the airplane, but you don't know the man what

made the air." I wished that day that I did know him, for I would most certainly have importuned him to calm the troubled waves. I struggled with my charge with misgivings as to my ability to ever get down anywhere.

The field—my home field—finally came in sight and I heaved a sigh of relief. I would at least be among friends when I hit the dirt. The motor grew gradually worse, having developed a decided cough which seemed to wrack her whole frame. Evidently the motor had decided that it would be much better to lie down and die among friends who could take care of her remains, for she gave up the ghost altogether a short distance from the field.

Here was the dread thing I had heard others talk about. Pilots of experience spoke in awed terms of serious crack-ups in forced landings and we came to fear them. Here I was faced with a forced landing on my own field and if I crashed—well, it might not be so bad, for some of my buddies would surely recognize the remains and I would not be long unidentified—and if I got away with it, I might be able to throw out my chest and brag with the chosen few who had had similar experiences. The chances of this latter coming true seemed very remote. Yet, I still had life and there was certainly hope. With a courage born of desperation and undoubtedly ignorance of just what a Jenny would do, I banked over and turned the nose in the general direction of the field. But where had it gone? It was here a moment ago. Oh, yes, there it is. I had turned quite sharply for a three-hour solo student and had become momentarily confused in my directions. The field was just ahead of me, but the familiar sock was stretched at right angles to my course into the field. What should I do? I scarcely had enough room to get into the field straight without trying to stretch my glide to carry me around the group of hangars which lined the near side of the field. Headquarters loomed up ahead and I knew that whatever happened in this particular affair, I would eventually land in that headquarters building, if alive. Consequently I had no desire just now to come in through the roof. I banked her over a bit and a large gold ball just grazed—well, nearly—my head. I had just missed the flagpole. I was all right now except for the fact that I was still headed cross-wind and still had to get past the two hangars. I decided to take chances on landing cross-wind for I was heading for the space between the two hangars.

It was inspection day—one of those days when the Commanding General and all his aides had decided to visit the camp in order to ascertain the progress of the Americans and report on the high quality of pilot material they found in our ranks. Here was my chance to raise the quality, and I would be the hero of the camp. That seemed to be my main concern now. So I struggled to get the old ship down and me out of it without any scratches. The flagpole had been left in the rear—there was no longer any risk of carrying the British flag down with me—I would now be able to walk in the front door of headquarters, for I was sure of at least getting on the field in some fashion. The next second I would be through the space between the hangars and wide open spaces would be before me.

That next second never came, for in some manner the fickle

god of luck which had previously been riding beside me to answer my every command, deserted me for some other admirer, and I suddenly stopped in both my thoughts and my forward progress. I was stuck hard and fast and elevated some twenty feet above the ground. I was still in the air, but my motor, ship and pilot were not flying. Nor were we doing any hangar flying either. I was up in the air in more ways than one. The hangar roof was a bit below me and too far to reach without crawling over the nose of the ship—and the ground was a sheer twenty feet below me—straight down. My knee, which had been sprained in an earlier crash, was not sufficiently strong enough to risk a jump. Anyhow, I was safe up here, and here I would remain until someone came up for me. Sometime later, with the assistance of several of my buddies who advised me to forsake flying and join the wrecking crew, I realized that I had passed the first two obstructions in fine shape, but the third, like the defenses of Leonidas at Thermopylae, refused to let me pass. My left wing had hooked in the hangar door support and held fast. This threw the nose around into the top of the support and it had stuck there much in the manner of a pen in a holder. It may not have been a clever landing for the British officers to write home about, but one of them admitted to me afterwards that it was the "most extraordinary" thing he had ever seen.

I was in a rather uncomfortable predicament (I almost decided to stay where I was until darkness would overtake me and I could slip down and hide away), for below me looking up in all seriousness—and with his familiar monocle set jauntily in his left eye—was the Adjutant of all the Royal Flying Corps squadrons in Canada. I had just wiped out one of his favorite ships or at least the salvage crew would finish the job when they tried to take it down from its perch. Finally a ladder was put up for me and I started my descent so rudely interrupted by the hangar some few minutes earlier. A few cheered, but saner heads prevailed and silence filled the air, to be suddenly rent asunder as though a cannon had boomed below me, "I say there, you, couldn't you see the 'angar?" The voice of the Adjutant was stentorious enough, but I almost dashed up the ladder again when I noticed the pained and unwelcome look on his face. I had seen the hangar, yes—I had seen several of them and I thought I had seen the one my ship was now resting against for the last time just before I would land safely on the airdrome.

I was almost constrained to reply to this leading question, but refrained because of the rank of my interrogator. Then again, there was the friendship of the British nation at stake. This time silence was golden, and without a word I strode to my quarters, after a dignified descent of the remaining rungs of the ladder, with the air of one who had suddenly, by his remarkable diplomacy, saved his country from a very embarrassing situation.

THE FLYING GENERAL

DURING the past year General James E. Fechet, Chief of the Air Corps, made flights to practically every state in the Union. He made one transcontinental flight and visited practically every Air Corps station in the country. Among others, a flight was made to the upper peninsula of Michigan, where landing fields are an unknown quantity. On one occasion during this flight it was necessary to land on a copper mine dump in a river bed. During this flight a 70-mile hop was made across Lake Michigan. When the General is on a cross-country flight, he usually follows the airline. In the far West he has flown an airline course across some of the most barren country in the United States—even across uninhabited deserts.

General Fechet's flying time for the year 1928 amounts to 397 hours and 15 minutes. During this time, he made flights in fourteen distinct types of airplanes, namely: O1; O2-H, Amphibian OA1C, O1-C, Thomas Morse XO-18, O2-J, Thomas Morse XO-19, O-11 (Observation), C-1, C-2 and C-3 (Transports), A-3, the Junkers Low-wing Monoplane and Sikorsky Amphibian. Several of his flights made during the year were especially significant, such as the flight from Washington, D. C., to Panama. This flight was made with Assistant Secretary of War F. Trubee Davison for the purpose of inspecting Air Corps activities in the Canal Zone. While on this trip, they visited every country in Central America. Needless to say, a large portion of this region is unpopulated, and the result of a forced landing can only be left to the imagination. The flight to Panama and return was made in amphibians. The difficulties encountered in attempting a flight of this nature may be appreciated from the fact that in the Central American countries there are practically no facilities for servicing an airplane. In other words, the crew was left entirely to its own devices and could look for no assistance.

Another of General Fechet's extended flights was the one to Greenly Island, Labrador, which was undertaken for the purpose of salvaging the transatlantic airplane *Bremen*.

This flight was also accomplished under difficulties, for a large portion of this country is likewise unpopulated. Facilities for the care of an airplane in these regions are unknown. Even though the flight was made in an amphibian plane and most of the flying was done over the water, icebergs and smaller pieces of ice which dotted the water presented a considerable hazard in case of a forced landing.

While on this flight, General Fechet once more displayed that quality which epitomizes the real aviator. In flying from St. George, New Brunswick, to Pictou, Nova Scotia, en route to Greenly Island, he found it necessary to make a land hop of about 60 miles over a range of mountains. Because this range of mountains was so heavily enshrouded with fog, three attempts to cross it proved unsuccessful. A landing was, therefore, made in the water near South Maitland, Nova Scotia, in the Bay of Fundy, at a time when the tide was going out with terrific force. The crews were able to anchor the ships only with considerable difficulty, the tide having been so strong that it dragged the anchors. The anchors finally took hold only a short distance from the banks of the bay. Shortly after this the anchor line of the accompanying ship broke because of the heavy pull of the tide. Capt. Ira C. Eaker, pilot of the accompanying ship, had but one thing left to do,—start the motor and try to get to Pictou.

Realizing that if the anchor line on the accompanying ship parted, his own line was apt to do likewise, and that if this happened the ship would be on the rocks before the motor could be started, General Fechet took immediate steps to prevent this contingency by attempting to get under way. The pull on the anchor line was so great that it was impossible to get the rope off the cleat on the bow of the ship. The only way, therefore, to free the amphibian from the anchor line was to cut the rope. This was done and the motor was started immediately. When taxiing out to the middle of the bay in order to take off, the plane ran aground at the exact place where Captain Eaker had previously taken off. Fifteen minutes after the plane ran aground the crew was walking around it on dry ground. The tide at this place is greater than anywhere else in the world. It is said that at times the tide is as great as 51 feet, which accounts for the swiftness of the water.

To wait for the return of the tide would have meant disaster. General Fechet foresaw this and avoided it in an unusual way. At this time, of course, the amphibian was high and dry as a boat; that is, the wheels were up. He set to work digging holes in the sand directly beneath the point where the wheels roll down. These holes were dug deep enough to allow the wheels to roll completely down. However, the weight of the ship was still on the hull. He then started to dig the sand from under the hull, allowing the weight of the ship then to be on the wheels. The amphibian was thus converted into a land-plane; that is, the weight was on the wheels and the tail skid. With the help of several men and by starting the motor, he was able to taxi out of the holes. He was then in a position to take off.

The General had accomplished a feat which had never been done before, or since that time; that is, he landed the amphibian as a seaplane and took it off as a landplane from exactly the same place. An hour following his take-off there would have been 30 feet of water at this place.

Although safely in the air, the General's troubles were not over. The fog was still in the mountains and, no longer having an anchor, he could not land on the water again. The only alternative was to fly to Pictou despite the fog. This was accomplished by flying directly over a small spur line railroad at an altitude of between 25 and 50 feet. In this way the land hop was accomplished, and his first interest upon arriving at Pictou was for the other ship. He gave a sigh of relief when he learned that Captain Eaker had landed safely about 20 miles away.

When on a cross-country flight or an expedition of any kind, the General is a real fellow, kicking in and doing his share of the work in the servicing and maintenance of the plane. General Fechet truly deserves the title of "The Flying General."

THE FLIGHT OF WILLIAMS AND YANCEY

BY CHARLES J. V. MURPHY

OF the many weird adventures recounted by trans-atlantic fliers—tales of fog that tortured the eyes and wearied the mind, tail spins in the black of night, and utter exhaustion—Roger Q. Williams and Lewis A. Yancey, who flew across the Atlantic, from Old Orchard, Maine, to Santander, Spain, and from there non-stop to Rome, have brought back the strangest story of all.

Said these young men: "We didn't have a single tail spin."

Said Yancey: "It was infernally dull."

Said Williams: "The quality of the Atlantic, like the quality of mercy, should not be strained. The air has been worse over Staten Island."

I asked Messrs. Williams and Yancey: "Then you aren't supermen at all?"

The two of them lifted their hands and chorused: "Gosh, no!"

It came about in this fashion. Williams and Yancey had their Bellanca Monoplane, *Pathfinder*, at Old Orchard, waiting for take-off weather. At 4:39 P.M., they received this telegram from that excellent gentleman, Dr. James A. Kimball, forecaster for fliers:

"Thunderstorms approaching from west. Will spread from Maine to Nova Scotia Monday, but preceded by freshening southwest winds. Start should be made before storm conditions reach Old Orchard. Much fog east to longitude 45. Less and thinner to southeast. Light but freshing winds mostly southwest of longitude 35, then fresh west to southwest longitude 15, then fresh west to northwest to coast."

Williams looked at the telegram and their weather map: "That's good," he said.

Yancey yelled: "Good? It's perfect."

They phoned the hangar on the beach, announced they were going in the morning. Benny Bauer, the Wright man, puttered around the Wright J-5, more out of love than need, for it was as sweet as an engine could be. The mechanics, Zabora and McCormick, went over the ship a last time. Harold Beadle, the Tidewater Oil expert, began ladling in 500 gallons of fuel. And Williams and Yancey went to bed.

They arose at 6:30, went down to the beach, noted with gladness that the tide was retreating, and the beach would soon be hard and firm. And the prospect of tail winds pleased them so mightily they decided to jettison 65 gallons of gas, to reduce the take-off load by nearly 400 pounds. It would be easier to get off.

At 8:30 o'clock Lieutenant Melko of the Coast Guard took off in an amphibian. Ten minutes later he dropped a note. "Visibility one-half a mile. Air good. Come on!" A light fog hung over the beach.

At 8:49, Williams and Yancey crawled into their ship, and took off. Williams was at the controls, and Yancey sat at his right.

* * *

It is unexpectedly easy, the take-off. The Bellanca lifts clear its load of 5,800 pounds in 3,000 feet. It climbs to 300 feet. Not caring to enter fog at that altitude, they circle in a cleared space until they reach 600 feet. Then Williams settles back in his chair—he has wisely equipped himself with a cushion —and heads for the compass course Yancey has set for Cape Sable.

The Coast Guard amphibian is tagging right along off the starboard; a flying boat carrying visitors from New York is off the port. So they journey for half an hour. Engine revolutions are dropped from 1,800 to 1,600. The altitude increases. The fog is still fairly thickish, and visibility is barely half a mile.

Williams reaches for the map, and scrawls on it: "We'll have an awful time flying blind with this load."

Yancey writes back: "Yeh, but what a nice party it would be with 550 gallons." He adds: "Better burn out some of the load first."

Williams tilts the nose slightly, and increases the angle of climb. At 2,000 feet they emerge above the fog, but the clouds are still above them. At 4,000 feet they are above the clouds, which lie, a perfect gray carpet, beneath them. Air speed is 85 miles an hour, a fresh southwest wind is nudging the tail. Perfect flying weather.

Yancey writes on the map: "Swell."

They are now flying blind—by instrument only. The solid layer of cloud insulates the ocean. Yancey, realizing they won't be able to sight Point Sable, shifts the course south. Decides to make it an all-water hop. He bends their course 600 miles below the Great Circle.

Williams is burning up the fuel in the wing tanks, and Yancey writes the caution: "Better keep the wing tanks full. If we get into trouble, we'll have gas to fly some place." Williams nods, and begins to pump fuel from the fuselage tanks to the wings.

"Doesn't seem to be a let-up in this fog," Williams writes.

But two hours later it does begin to break up. Holes appear, and through them they see water—their first glimpse of it since they started. They sight a tramp steamer, nearly a mile below them, a black spot in a hole of gray.

Only a few low clouds remain by this time; the air is perfectly calm, and so is the sea. "Do you think we can get by at night if we hit low clouds?" Yancey writes. Williams smiles and wiggles his fingers, to show them spinning down. "Cheerful thought," Yancey jots in reply.

Presently they run into low clouds, and the ocean becomes obscured. The Whirlwind is roaring nicely. Except for the clouds, which lie in two layers, above and below, conditions are perfect.

Yancey studies them, and writes to Williams: "I think they will clear up soon. Two layers never last long."

And so they continue. Sunset steals up behind them, over the left wing. It advances very slowly. Behind are the painted clouds, and ahead a sky changing from golden gray to rich purple, and then to black. This is the most ticklish moment for them, and they concentrate on the instruments, Williams flying and Yancey checking on the fluttering fingers on the dials. As the horizon melts and becomes ocean, blind flying becomes a fine art. There is no fixed point upon which to balance the ship.

But having practiced in anticipation of just this situation, Yancey and Williams soon surrender their watchfulness; neither has any difficulty in maintaining the course. Twilight fades into night, and the brightest stars flicker up ahead. They switch on the dashboard light, and Williams yawns.

"Do you figure our speed at 115?" he asks—on the map.

Yancey nods. "We must have a wonderful tail wind!" he jots in reply.

An hour after darkness came on, Williams turns over the controls to Yancey, climbs on the fuel tank, sinks a pillow under his head, rolls himself in a comforter, and goes to sleep. Two hours pass. It is pitch dark; the moon is in the last quarter, and cannot be seen. But Yancey has little difficulty in following his course. The tachometer now shows 1,550 revolutions per minute, and the altimeter 8,000 feet.

It nears midnight. A squeak puzzles him, but he cannot locate it. The tachometer cuts out. So that was it! Yancey concentrates on the air-speed indicator. And then the earth indicator compass, with a few weird gyrations, goes to pot and joins the tachometer in its droll by-play.

Blind flying becomes a bit too complicated. Yancey reaches

up, gathers what little of Williams' retreating hair is available, and yanks vigorously. Williams stifles a yawn, rubs his eyes, and moans: "What the ——! G'wan and fly it yourself." But he takes over the controls.

"Do you think," Yancey writes, "I can crawl back to the tank?" Williams nods.

Yancey crawls back, flashlight in hand, and removes the cover of the generator operating the earth inductor compass. He has just replaced it when he feels Williams rock the wings—a signal to return. He crawls back, and Williams points toward the steering compass. It, too, has caved in.

"We can't repair any of them," Yancey shouts. "We'll have to use the seat compass." It is the compass set in the seat between them, which they have provided for just such an emergency. Fortunately, it is unaffected by the demise of the others. Yancey returns to the controls, and Williams, not a little offended by what he terms "this unnecessary interruption," goes back to sleep.

About two o'clock he replaces Yancey, who scrambles atop the gas tank, pulls down the trap-door and "sights" the stars. The weather continues beautiful; a fading fragment of the moon is visible dead behind. They are 8,000 feet high. Far below a transatlantic steamer unveils a galaxy of lights.

It is 72 degrees warm in the cabin, although the outside temperature reads 40. They remove their heavy flying jackets and helmets, and open their shirt collars.

"Darn hot this time of the year," writes Williams. "Wish we had brought along summer underwear."

Dawn comes in very slowly. The sky becomes a rich pearl gray, and a red sun pops up directly athwart the dejected compass. As the horizon evolves, they watch their instruments more carefully, until they get their bearings. Then everything is fine.

"A gray dawn," Yancey writes. "Sign of a good day."

An unbroken carpet of clouds unfurls ahead of them. The ocean is not visible. Their altitude is 8,000 feet, and the upper cloud layer about 4,000 feet below. They make ready for breakfast—and, after an appraisal of the commissary stores, choose a bar of chocolate, coffee and an orange each.

Williams jerks his thumb toward the delicatessen roast chicken, and writes: "I never had a chicken for breakfast before, and I'd better not start now."

He sees, presently, a patch of ocean, and writes: "Do you know this is the first time I've ever been out to sea?"

Yancey stares at him: "Suffering cats, why didn't you tell me that before!"

They regret their forgetfulness in not bringing along shaving supplies, but change their shirts and collars. "Nothing like a clean shirt in the morning," Roger yells. "Sets you right up."

The altitude of the clouds increases; by nine o'clock the crests of the highest are on line with the inwgs. Yancey pulls back on the stick a bit. They reach their ceiling—11,000 feet—and skim over the barrier.

Plotting his position, Yancey is gratified to note that the west southwest tail wing is continuing, giving them an added speed of about 25 miles an hour, and an air speed of 110 miles an hour at three-quarters throttle.   "Doc. Kimball knows his stuff," he writes on the map.

The clouds begin to break up; by noon the sky is only partly cloud, and the weather holds good.

"How long do you think these clouds will last? To the Coast?" Williams writes.

"About that," Yancey replies.   He sets his course for a point 20 miles north of Cape Ortegal, on the northwest coast of Spain. He estimates its distance then at 600 miles.

The afternoon wears on, and they sight several cargo steamers, all too far beneath them to hear their engine.   About five o'clock Yancey changes the course to round Cape Ortegal and parallel to the coast.   A terrific thunderhead looms up off the starboard, 15,000 feet of hell-making clouds.

"Looks like a real storm in there," he writes.   "Glad we didn't hit it in the dark."

About an hour later they head southeast in order to sight the Spanish coast, now quite near.   Fifteen minutes later they sight it 12 miles away—a rough headland rising out of the sea.   They are now just east of Cape Ortegal.

They head parallel to the shore again, holding a course five to ten miles off shore.   "We will get the water distance record," Yancey writes, "if we land at Bayonne."

The two of them calculate their gas supply, and come to the conclusion there isn't enough left to carry them through the night to Rome.   To continue means risking a forced landing, perhaps in the dark.   They had requested the officials at the airports at Toulouse, Bayonne and Marseilles to be on the watch for them, but there was no way of learning whether these fields were equipped for night landings. Yancey scrawls a message on the map: "Suggest we land in the daylight, refuel and continue at once for Rome." Williams favors the idea. About 7:30 o'clock, they head in for the shore, seeking a likely landing place.

Yancey writes: "Try one of these beaches."

They nose in, and find a village near the shore.

They come down very easily—touching earth after 31 hours, 30 minutes in the air, after having flown 3,439 miles over water without once sighting land. It was a new long-distance water record for aircraft.

"Well," announced Roger Williams, touching earth himself, "that's over."

* * *

After that, our young business men stayed in Santander overnight, having found it impossible to get aviation gas before morning, and they were royally entertained. About noontime the next day—the 10th—they took off for Rome, landing in the famous city about ten o'clock at night, and accomplishing, among other celebrated things, the phenomenal feat of keeping Mussolini waiting for more than two hours.

FLAMING GAS BEACONS?

BY EARLE OVINGTON

IT was just dusk when I left my airport at Santa Barbara, California, to go to Long Beach, an air distance of about one hundred miles. It was pitch dark, of course, by the time I got halfway there.

Passing over the Santa Monica hills, and a few minutes later leaving Clover Field on my starboard side and Roger's on my port, I looked around for the rotating beacon which I knew was in operation on the municipal airport of Long Beach.

The night was clear and, knowing this locality pretty well, I had no difficulty in spotting Long Beach, but no rotating beacon stood out among the sea of lights which comprise the night illumination of this city of oil wells. Large lights, small lights; white lights, yellow lights, red lights; steady lights and blinking lights; thousands of lights of every description and color. But I could not, for the life of me, pick out anything that I could identify as a rotating airport beacon. It was not until I was literally within three miles of the Long Beach airport that I was able to pick up its beacon.

Lest you think that the beacon at Long Beach is inadequate in size I hasten to assure you that it is as large as most, and larger

than many.   It was only because it is surrounded by the lights
of the city—and Long Beach believes in using electricity for
advertising purposes—that makes it so difficult to distinguish
from the air.

Ah, what is that?   A pillar of fire up against the foothills on
my left!   The burning oil well at Sante Fe Springs, of course.

What a beacon!   In color, contour, and size, unlike any other
light in the sea of lights which stretched below me on all sides.

"Why not a flaming gas beacon for airports?" flashed through
my mind; and since then I've repeatedly asked myself this
question.   Yes, why not?

The obvious construction would be a pylon, or tower, resembling an oil derrick, of steel, from the top of which would project
a tube from which would issue the flaming gas.   Far above the
earth, as this flame would be, there would be no fire hazard.

The lurid reddish-yellow color of flaming gas is unlike that of
any electric light; in shape it is entirely different from any other
source of illumination; and its size is greater than that of any
other light.   In actual candle power the flaming gas beacon is not
a powerful light, but the size of the actual source of illumination
is relatively great.

For these reasons the flaming gas beacon would be far more
easily distinguished among a myriad of other lights than any
other form of similar device.

Furthermore, a point which I had almost forgotten, the long
wave-lengths of light issuing from a flaming gas beacon would
penetrate fog and mist to a much greater extent than the comparatively short wave-lengths of the ordinary electric beacon.

I am aware of the fact that the airport beacon usually serves two purposes: first, it enables the pilot to locate the field; and second, it tells the pilot which field it is. In other words, the light of the beacon attracts the pilot's attention and the sequence of the flashes, or the time between flashes, indicates upon which field the beacon is located.

In the case of the flaming gas beacon, the light could be cut off intermittently with a rotating shield and thus serve the same two purposes, but this would greatly impair the efficiency of the beacon. The gas could even be turned up and down automatically and accomplish the same object. A better arrangement, it seems to me, would be to have as large a flaming gas beacon as possible to attract attention to the field and, at another point on the field, a smaller electric beacon which would indicate the name of the field.

Some cities, such as Long Beach, are blowing off millions of cubic feet of natural illuminating gas into the air just because the supply is so far in excess of the demand. For these communities the cost of fuel for the flaming gas beacon would be negligible.

In many localities, on the other hand, natural gas is not available and artificial illuminating gas is expensive, if obtainable at all. But oil is portable and comparatively cheap in any section of the country and could be sprayed into the air, from some atomizing device, and serve as fuel for the flaming gas beacon which I am advocating.

Referring to the flaming oil well at Sante Fe Springs, which first put this idea into my head, I realize that no artificial beacon could be of such high intrinsic brilliancy since the consumption of fuel would be prohibitive.   When I came to study the flame, however, as I did by flying round it for over half an hour, I came to the conclusion that a much smaller flame of the same character would adequately serve the purpose.   It was not so much the size or brilliancy of the flame which made it stand out so prominently as it was its character; its dissimilarity as compared with the surrounding electric lights.

If the lights of a city were all steady, a rotating beacon would not be so difficult to distinguish; but there are so many flashing signs used for advertising purposes that the intermittent airport beacon is just one of a large number of blinking sources of illumination.   The flaming gas beacon would give a light of an entirely different character and therefore be more readily distinguished.

AERIAL POST OFFICES NOW PRACTICAL

BOEING Airplane Company announces its tri-motored eighteen-passenger transports can be easily adapted for aerial Post Office service. When the Post Office Department decides to move all first-class mail, between certain cities, by air, using planes with facilities for sorting clerks, the Boeing transcontinental eighteen-passenger planes, now nearing completion at the Boeing plant, will be adapted for that purpose, officials announce. The planes can carry more than three tons of mail or a quarter of a million letters at a high speed of 135 miles an hour.

Boeing engineers announce that, with few minor alterations, these planes can be transformed into the much talked-of aerial post offices. The cabins are nineteen and one-half feet long and a six-foot sorting clerk can stand upright and have room to spare. The width of the cabin is five and one-half feet. These planes have a wing span of eighty feet and length overall of fifty-five feet.

Letter carriers can have their meals aboard the planes, which are equipped with small buffet. They also have a fully equipped lavatory, with hot and cold running water.

The planes have special night-flying equipment, and radio telephone, permitting pilots to talk to ground stations 200 miles distance, will be installed.

261

WIRELESS FOR LIGHT AEROPLANES

A LIGHT-WEIGHT wireless telephone set for use on light aeroplanes has been designed by the Marconi Company to enable owner-pilots and clubmen to communicate while in flight with ground stations, as is done by commercial passenger-carrying aircraft.

The weight of the new set, known as the Marconi Type A.D.22, has been reduced to about 60 pounds. It combines a telephone transmitter and receiver in a compact wooden box measuring only 16 by 7 inches, and the total weight includes complete equipment with all accessories, such as microphone and telephones, wind-driven generator, accumulator, aerial, and connecting leads. It may thus be easily carried in all the popular types of light aeroplanes.

The "A.D.22" has been designed for the transmission of telephony only, as experience shows that the pilot, even if he is well acquainted with the Morse code, is usually sufficiently occupied in flying the machine and watching his instruments without being expected to concentrate on telegraph signals.

Although the set is a "miniature" in respect to size and weight, its performance is well suited to the requirements of the flying

tourist.   With a power of 75 watts—equivalent to that used by
many ordinary domestic electric lamps—the transmitter will
cover ranges of 50 to 75 miles when communicating with the
normal class of aerodrome ground stations, while with efficient
ground stations such as Croydon, ranges up to 100 miles are easily
attainable.   The reception range from modern aerodrome transmitters considerably exceeds these distances, and the receiver
is, of course, capable of intercepting telegraph signals, both
continuous wave and interrupted continuous wave, as well as
telephony.

The set can be installed for operation by the passenger,
or it may be fitted in any convenient part of the machine
and operated by the pilot through a remote control unit,
the tuning having been simplified to "one handle" manipu-
lation.

For normal working the wave range of the transmitter and
receiver is 850 to 950 metres, this being the international aircraft wave band, but a quick-change switch is provided to
enable the 600-metre ships' wave-length to be employed in
emergency.

The amateur pilot is now enabled to take advantage of the
wireless facilities for aircraft that are widely employed in commercial aviation, an advance that is highly desirable in view of
rapidly increasing popularity of private air cruising on business
and pleasure.   Advice regarding weather ahead, state of the
various aerodromes, and other information is made available
to light aeroplane tourists, and in addition they are provided
with a valuable means of position finding when flying over the

Continent and other parts of the world where there are aerodrome ground stations equipped with wireless direction finders. The importance attached to these services by aviation authorities is demonstrated by the fact that international regulations now in force practically throughout the world require all passenger-carrying commercial aircraft to be equipped with an adequate wireless installation.

Lacking wireless the pilot is compelled to land to obtain information, recurring additional charges and possibly considerable delay.

The principal reason for the limited use of wireless by private owners of light aeroplanes up to the present has been the fact that the wireless equipment designed and manufactured for use in commercial aircraft is usually too large and too heavy for light aeroplanes. While it was therefore necessary to design the new set along entirely new lines, the "A.D.22" embodies the wide experience of the Marconi Company in the manufacture of its standard aircraft sets, which are in regular use in civil, military, and naval aircraft in more than thirty countries and are standard equipment in all Imperial Airways machines.

DETAILS OF COMPONENTS

The essential components of the transmitter and receiver are mounted in a light wooden box with strong lugs to which rubber shock absorbers can be attached when the set is fitted in the machine. The transmitter comprises an aerial tuning inductance with adjustments and switch for 900 and 600 metre wavelengths, an oscillation valve, Type M.T.5, for energizing the aerial circuit by means of a variable reaction coil, and an anode tap connection on the aerial tuning inductance, and a modulating system consisting of a control valve, Type, M.T.5., connected in series with a speech choke.

The principal components of the receiver are a tuner, with slow motion condenser adjustment for high frequency selection; a single stage of screened-grid, high frequency magnification with valve, Type S.610; a detector, with capacity reaction and valve, Type D.E.L.610, and a low frequency magnification stage with valve, Type D.E.L.610. The circuits employed in the receiver have been specially developed to insure simplicity of operation, "one handle" tuning, smooth reaction, and a high degree of selectivity and sensitivity.

The microphone and telephones are designed for aeroplane work and are practically unaffected by engine noises.

A generator of small and light construction provides both high and low tension current for the transmitter and receiver, the high tension output being 1,000 volts, 75 milliamperes, and the low tension output being 7 volts, 4 amps. It is fitted with a constant speed windmill which is self-regulating over a range of wind speeds from 70 to 170 miles per hour, thus insuring a constant power supply.

NEVER HAS BEEN AIRPLANE ENGINE

BY HENRY FORD

IN all the development of aviation there has never been a real airplane engine. The perfection of an engine designed especially for flying is now one of the most important pieces of research being carried out in our plants.

Today there is no such thing in existence as an airplane engine. What we call airplane engines are really automobile engines in all their fundamental principles. Some of our experiments here at Dearborn may help discover what an airplane engine should be. At present we are giving our attention to the Diesel engine. The outlook is fairly promising.

The young mind and every mind, must get together to produce the airplane engine of the future. No one knows now just what it will be like but you can be pretty sure that it will have four characteristics: First, low speed; second, reliability; third, perfect balance; fourth, it will use a fuel that will be four or five times more powerful than our present fuel. By the time the engine that will meet these requirements is ready, we may have a type of plane that can come down and make a landing at a speed considerably less than sixty miles an hour.   That is where one of the big human factors enters in.   People won't stand for the hazard of a sixty-mile-an-hour landing.

The type of plane capable of landing at a much slower speed has got to come if the airplane is going to accomplish all that we have a right to expect of it.

I see a greater future for young men in aviation than in any other field.   If the young man of today wants to tie up with something that has a good future, he will go after the airplane. The airplane is going to need lots of help.   As I have said, the first thing he ought to do is to find out what has been done to bring the airplane to its present phase and then recognize that the present phase is only a very early stage.

Boys who are thinking about airplanes now do so without even knowing what kind of an engine an airplane ought to have. It reminds me of the time when I was starting.   I was then thinking in terms of steam because steam was in use in locomotives.   It was only after much experimenting that I turned to the gas engine.

It is perfectly natural that boys should think that airplanes should run with gas engines.   They think so because automobiles are run by gas engines.   But some day a boy will come along who will discover that gas engines are not the thing at all.

PEGASUS, "THE FLYING HORSE"

How to Build and Fly This Remarkable Model

BY R. E. DOWD

THIS time we are returning to model building by taking up the design and construction of a most unusual flying model. It is quite a step from the "Yardsticker" sailplane, already described, to the Pegasus, but since many are interested in plans of a more advanced type, here they are.

Pegasus, as you may know, was the flying horse of Greek mythology, and it may seem a strange name for a modern airplane, but here's how it all came about. Mr. Agnew E. Larsen, chief engineer of the Pitcairn Aircraft Corporation, when examining the model, exclaimed: "What's the idea of the four wheels? It stands up like a horse." That was enough to give the idea, and it was promptly christened "Pegasus—the flying horse."

Perhaps you have made some of the ultra light and fragile models which must be flown in a calm and have been disappointed in their limited possibilities. Models of this type have remarkable durations because of their light weight, but for everyday, reliable performance, they cannot be called dependable. That's why we have Pegasus. With its high center of gravity, dihedral and sweptback wing, its pusher propeller, and its rugged tubular fuselage, the Pegasus will fly into mean, gusty winds; climb to great heights, cover distances of a quarter mile, and fly day after day without a sign of breakage.

The design suggested itself from a study of Mr. Fokker's first airplane called "The Spider." It had the same wing form and center of gravity location, and its stability was so great that no ailerons or lateral balancing devices were employed. With its great ungainly stick projecting out forward, the Pegasus is anything but a beauty, but once in the air, it flies with exceptional stability and grace.

That's the story of the Pegasus. Now let's build it. It is not very difficult. Just make up your mind to do a really fine job before you begin, and you will never regret building the Pegasus.

Here's what you need for materials:

1. 1/32 inch thick basswood for fuselage and ribs.
2. White pine for propeller blank and end plugs.
3. 3/32 inch by ¼ inch white pine or basswood for wing spars.
4. Bamboo for wing tips and tail.
5. Sheet aluminum for wing spar joint and front fin.
6. Rubber strand for motor.
7. 1/16 inch diameter plane wire for propeller shaft and hooks.
8. Wire for trailing edge of plane and landing gear.
9. Dress snaps for wing mounting.
10. Wheels.
11. One release dog from an old alarm clock and 2 inches 3/32 O.D. brass tubing.
12. Rice paper and a small piece of silk.
13. Banana oil, Ambroid cement, soldering shellac, equipment.

Build the Fuselage First

The fuselage is 36 inches long and is formed of 1/32 inch thick selected basswood. The sheet of wood is first reinforced by an application of rice paper doped on with banana oil. Before attempting to wrap the wood around the ¾ inch diameter paraffined dowel, which is used as a form, you immerse it in fairly hot water. A few seconds of this immersion will soften the wood so that it can be easily formed. The surface to which the paper is doped is, of course, used as the inside, and the paper then becomes a reinforcing lining. The wood will be found to be so soft and pliable that it readily forms around the dowel. String or rubber strand will hold it to the shape of the dowel while drying.

When it is thoroughly dry, the wrapping is removed and the edges trimmed and beveled for cementing. Allow about ¼ inch for overlap and then slip the shell over the paraffined dowel again, this time applying Ambroid to the lap joint and wrapping with rubber strand. Before the cement sets, twist the tube about one turn by twisting the ends in opposite directions. This will avoid any distortion of the tube from the cemented joint. When thoroughly dry, the dowel can be easily removed by heating slightly, which will melt the paraffin. A final coat of rice paper doped on makes a three-ply fuselage of great strength and beauty.

The front and rear ends of the fuselage are reinforced in exactly the same manner, so that a description of one will apply to the other. A white pine plug liner ¼ inch thick is fitted snugly and glued to the inside of the tube. It has a 7/16 inch square hole

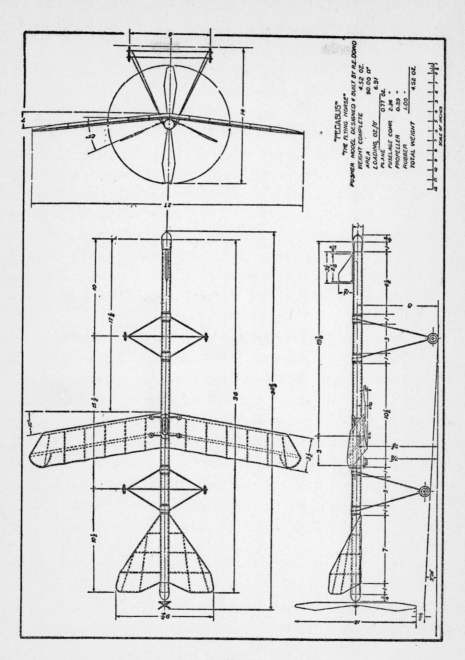

"PEGASUS"
"THE FLYING HORSE"
PUSHER MODEL DESIGNED & BUILT BY R.E. DOWD

WEIGHT COMPLETE	4.52 OZ.	
AREA	90.00 □"	
LOADING, OZ./□'	6.91	
PLANE	0.77 OZ.	
FUSELAGE COMP?	2.36 "	
PROPELLER	0.39 "	
RUBBER	1.00 "	
TOTAL WEIGHT	4.52 OZ.	

SCALE OF INCHES

271

in it to receive the streamline end plug, which is also of white pine. The outside reinforcing collar is 7/8 inch diameter tapering to nothing in a length of 1 inch. It can be easily made from an extra piece of the fuselage material cut off before cementing the tube seam. It fits the tube snugly and is cemented in position. The anchor hook for the rubber strand passes through the nose block. In order to prevent its turning, it is bent in the form of a loop and pulled into the block. A brad driven through both the block and the loop completes the unit. The outer end is formed into an eye so as to accommodate the winder hook. The rubber is wound by hooking directly to the block. This eliminates the hooking and unhooking of the highly tensioned rubber, a task which is often attended with mishaps, especially in cold weather. With this arrangement, the nose plug is simply allowed to draw back into position where its square shank takes the torsion of the rubber. The convenience of this system will be appreciated by all who have had experience in winding models with the rubber hooked up in the usual manner, requiring transferring from winder to frame.

The rear block, in which the propeller bearing is mounted, is identical to the nose block. The bearing is made of brass tubing which is approximately 3/32 inch outside diameter. The inside diameter is such as to provide a good running fit with the .063 steel wire propeller shaft. The bearing tube is allowed to protrude slightly through the block, where it takes the thrust from a thrust collar soldered to the propeller shaft. See sketch of thrust collar, which is nothing more than a piece of tubing 1/8 inch long of the same size as used for the bearing.

NEXT BUILD THE WING

The main wing has both a pronounced sweepback and a dihedral. For this reason it is constructed in two units, the right and left sections, which are assembled together afterwards by four .032 aluminum plates 3/16 inch wide and 1 inch long, which are cut to the angle of sweepback and bent to the dihedral angle, and then lashed to the top and bottom of each spar. This method of joining is simple, as well as strong and light. Both spars are basswood, 3/32 inch thick and ¼ inch wide. The front spar forms the leading edge of the wing, and its edge is consequently rounded slightly to conform to the rib section, which is cut from 1/32 inch thick basswood to Eiffel No. 35 section. This airfoil was used originally by the Wright brothers on their historic biplanes.

The rear surface of the front spar is notched 1/32 inch deep to receive the ribs which butt up against it. Attachment is accomplished by simply ambroiding the ribs in place. The joint at the rear spar is, however, slightly more difficult to make. It might be called a half-lap joint, but the spar is really notched about ¾ inch of its depth from the top, and the ribs are notched

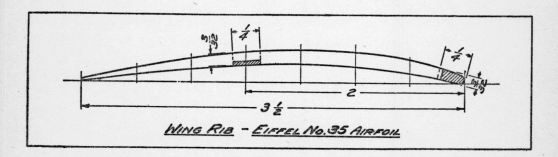

WING RIB – EIFFEL No. 35 AIRFOIL

the remaining ¼ inch.   A ¼-inch wide strip of .010 sheet aluminum ¾ inch long is lashed on the top surface of the rear spar at each joint.   This serves to strengthen the spar where it has been weakened by notching.   After the joint has been thoroughly cemented, both the spar and ribs will be found to be as strong as though they had not been notched.

The wing ends are of bamboo 1/16 inch square, which is lashed to the front spar and is formed around the rear spar and end rib in a smooth curve.   This is done in order to strengthen the end rib against the tension of the fine steel wire trailing edge and also protect it from end shocks on the wing tip.   The wire used for the trailing edge is given a single turn around the rib ends.   A touch of cement on this makes a simple and reliable fastening.

The top surface of the two center panels is covered with silk, but the remainder of the wing is covered with Japanese rice paper doped on with banana oil.   By using care this can be applied without allowing the surfaces to stick together.   If the surfaces should accidentally stick together while doping, they can be quickly separated by neatly punching a small hole in the paper and blowing the breath into the wing while the dope is still soft.   For mounting the wing the male parts of four medium-sized dress snaps are lashed to the top surface of the spars, preferably after covering.   They are spaced 2⅝ inches apart on centers.   These serve to attach the wing to the steel wire struts of the wing hanger.   This hanger is composed of a mounting plate, a name plate, two wire struts, and the four female parts of the dress snaps.   The mounting plate is of sheet tin, ⅞ inch wide by 2¼ inches long.   A large lightening hole, 11/16 inch wide and 1¾ inches long, is cut in the plate and the aluminum name plate, which, of course, is simply a novelty, is riveted on so that the name "Pegasus" is quite conspicuous.   The popularity that a model enjoys, once its name becomes known among the junior "fans," is certainly surprising and well repays the builder for the small amount of additional work required to add this feature.

The wire struts are made of .032 steel wire.   They are soldered to the tin mounting plate and their ends are bent after annealing so that they form loops or eyes into which the dress snaps are soldered.   By bending the wire struts, the angle of incidence may be changed.   It will be found that an incidence of 4 degrees, however, will give the best results.   The covering is Japanese rice paper, except the top surface of the two center panels which is silk to prevent puncturing.   Both the paper and the silk are doped with banana oil.

Now the Stabilizer

The stabilizer frame is constructed entirely of bamboo.   The ribs, both lateral and longitudinal, are 1/32 inch thick by 1/16 inch wide.   The outline is 1/32 inch square and is formed to the required shape over a flame.   On the original model this outline was a single piece, but because of the difficulty of making the reverse bend in the "V" of the tail, it is advisable to make it in two pieces.   The frame is built with an unusually large dihedral angle which avoids the necessity of a rear fin and improves longitudinal stability.   Double surfacing of doped Japanese rice paper is used as a covering.   The finished stabilizer is fastened to the fuselage by lashing with thread.

The Fin is Next

A fin made from .010 thick sheet aluminum is provided on the nose of the model. The attachment of a sheet metal fin to the fuselage of a model is an item of construction that has given model builders much trouble. Because of the simplicity and success of the method used on the Pegasus, it seems advisable to describe it in detail.

The fin, after being cut to size, is stamped on its lower edge by a row of small depressions made by a center punch against a hard wood block. Successive depressions are made from opposite sides of the fin in order to preserve its symmetry. A 1/16 inch by ¼ inch basswood mounting strip is slotted and recessed on its underside to receive the fin which is inserted from the bottom. The unit, fin and mounting strip, is assembled on to the fuselage. Cement is used liberally so that it fills in around the depressions and unites the whole into a firm, reliable mounting. The rear edge of the fin may be bent to steer the model. This method of steering will be found very effective because of the great distance between the center of gravity and the fin.

Now Make the Landing Gear

The undercarriage of this model is made up of two units that are identical except for the length of the wire struts. These struts are made of .030 steel music wire. Each set is made of a single piece of wire joined by a soldered lap joint. This joint occurs under the streamline caps, which are simply pieces of the fuselage tube after cutting to length. These caps are fitted snugly over the struts and are cemented and lashed to the fuselage. A through axle of the same diameter as the struts mounts the

1-inch diameter celluloid wheels. The axle is wrapped with fine wire and soldered into the apex of the "V" struts. Small aluminum washers on either side of the wheel and a bent-up axle end are all that is necessary to complete the undercarriage.

CARVING THE PROPELLER IS NEXT

Although in outline the propeller resembles closely the historic Lang propeller, it is really radically different. Its pitch is not uniform but reduces from the point of maximum blade width to the hub. This condition is caused by the rather unusual reduction in blank thickness near the hub. See drawing of blank. The carving is simple and easily done. The finished propeller is extremely neat and is among the most efficient I have ever tested. The blank is of white pine, and the whole propeller is covered

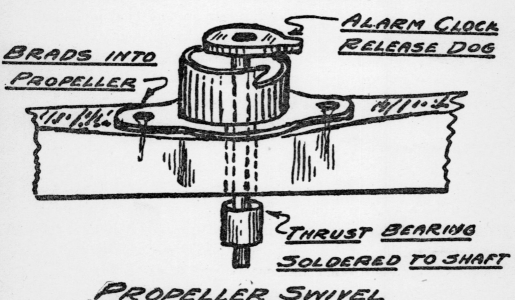

BRADS INTO PROPELLER

ALARM CLOCK RELEASE DOG

THRUST BEARING SOLDERED TO SHAFT

PROPELLER SWIVEL

with Japanese rice paper, which is doped on after carving and sanding. Though not absolutely necessary, a swivel attachment of the propeller will greatly increase the length of flights by prolonging the glide. The release dog from an alarm clock can be easily adapted as shown in the sketch. Note that the entire tension of the rubber is taken on the thrust bearing soldered to the shaft.

About one ounce of rubber strand is used to power the Pegasus. The rubber is kept well lubricated, and because of its complete enclosure in the tube, the usual trouble of picking up grit on landing is eliminated. The reduction of air resistance due to the enclosed rubber is responsible to a great extent for the performance of this model.

READY TO FLY

When everything is all trued up and adjusted, try the balance by gliding the model without power. It should balance with the wing located as shown. However, if the wing hanger is fastened by wrapping with rubber strands, adjustments will be

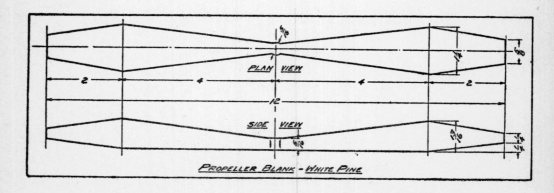

possible by shifting the wing forward or rearward.   Remember if it noses up, move the wing back, and vice versa.

Although I have flown hundreds of models, I have never known any that had such a consistently reliable performance as the Pegasus.   Its record of successful service covers, not weeks or months, but years, in which time it has doubtless covered several hundred miles air distance.   In R.O.G. flights, the take-off is slow and because of this, the length of such flights is con-siderably less than when hand-launched.

The start, either hand-launched or R. O. G., is invariably made cross-wind so that the wind acting under the main plane dihedral resists the turning action of the torque until it "finds" itself in the air.   The model usually rises quickly to a height of one to two hundred feet, where it straightens out and either bucks prevailing winds or circles until its power is exhausted.   The glide is made at an angle of one in four, the propeller swiveling freely, which makes it difficult for the inexperienced to determine at what point the power became exhausted.

BIGGER AND BETTER BALLOONS

BY DON ROSE

THE tensile strength of my air-minded imagination has been sorely tested during the past week or so.* There has been right smart "goings-on" in the air, so that I feel just now like a small boy with a stiff neck at a three-ring circus. I don't remember that anyone officially appointed this as Aviation Week, but if they had they would now be patting themselves on the back for a highly successful performance.

There was, for instance, the nice little military demonstration out in the Middle West. There were the Washington meetings, whereat Harold Pitcairn turned up in the Autogiro and left the industry mildly goggle-eyed and looking for alibis. The flying windmill took its first long trip in this country and back again, clocking the course at 110 miles an hour and alighting at both ends with a landing run of at least three feet. That was something, if you ask me. There was also the Packard petroleum engine, which flew into Langley Field under wraps and stayed that way until it had aroused a thousand columnar miles of newspaper curiosity. I gather that it was supposed to be a secret, which is why two newspaper correspondents were granted a peep at it. If you want to keep

June, 1929.

something as secret as the time of day, tell it to two newspaper correspondents.

On top of all this, with additional entertainment from one airport convention, an altitude record, a woman's endurance record, thirteen new airports and a few thousand miles more of air-mail service, the *Graf Zeppelin* stuck its nose out over the Atlantic looking for Lakehurst, where most of the population of the eastern United States was gathering to greet it and to eat hot dogs in rolls modeled more or less along the lines of its classic contours. It was too bad indeed that they were disappointed, and a tough break for the *Graf* and her commander and crew. The only consolation in the situation is that real tragedy was cheated by good sense and caution. The passengers should have little to complain about, even though they were all looking forward to a serene and enjoyable crossing and a Saturday evening dinner in New York City, including that persistent patron of the international radio-telephone, Mrs. Pierce. Mr. Pierce, it seems, was not so keen about it, probably because he looks forward now to a future in which he will be known only as the husband of Mrs. Pierce, sole lady passenger on the second commercial flight by air. I am not counting, you see, the lady gorilla, who seems to have been some sort of official chaperon, nor the grand piano which was carried along for no reason that any expert has yet explained. The aeronautical implications of a grand piano are still beyond me, but I suppose somebody had to carry a grand piano by airship and get it over with. There is still to come the airship wedding, the airship bridge party, and the airship tennis match, but after a while all the old publicity stunts will have gone safely through their second incarnation and we shall be able to get down to business.

There was, it is true, some delay in getting away from Europe on this second trip, but for this no sensible bystander will bring blame or complaint. It was pretty well hammered into the public's head that this was a business trip and a commercial crossing, and in no sense a stunt or pioneer demonstration of what an airship could do with the aid of luck and good weather. There were passengers on board who had paid for safe passage regardless of the thrill and novelty of holding a ticket on the first airliner. Since the ocean is wide and wet, the Commander chose to play safe rather than be sorry, and to turn back while the repair shop was still within reach. It was too bad, but the only real sufferers were the tens of thousands of hot dogs that went stale at Lakehurst, and no doubt science and the ingenuity of man found something to do with them.

The commercial implications of the *Graf's* second trip gave it its real importance. The rigid airships are making this year their bid for business. It is, to be sure, their turn. The airplane got off at a fast pace during the latter years of the war, and has dominated the skies ever since. It was not always thus. In the earlier days of the great unpleasantness, the Zeppelins had things pretty much their own way, and it was, in fact, their troublesome presence that did much to stimulate airplane design to the point where planes could outclimb and outmaneuver the airships and shoot them full of incendiary bullets, which spoiled them quite a little. This in turn stimulated defensive technique, so that the aviation experts of all nations sharpened their wits on each other for three or four years of war, and boosted along the plane's progress at an amazing clip. But let it not be supposed that the authorities thereby lost sight of the airship's possibilities. If they had done so, they would not have thrown so many post-war restrictions around Germany's construction of rigid aircraft. Only lately have these restrictions been lightened, and the first consequence is the *Graf*, the biggest ship that could be built at the time in the biggest shed in Germany.

It is interesting to note that bigger and better airships is the slogan of the development of lighter-than-air craft. The *Graf* is considerably bigger than the *Los Angeles;* the new British airships will be half as big again; the two now being built at Akron for the U. S. Navy will top everything in sight by a million and a half cubic feet. This is not the consequence of any competitive desire to own the biggest balloon in the world. It is a matter of efficiency and safety. The bigger the ship, the more weight it can carry in proportion to its bulk and power, and the less likely it is to crack under the strain of service. In this respect the airship has an edge—for the present at least—on the airplane. The load capacity of a plane steps right along with the horsepower needed to fly it, and after a certain point the useful load begins to vanish altogether. Those who draw the pretty pictures for the Sunday supplements sometimes forget this, but the designers don't. For the present, at least, there is a limit beyond which the airplane becomes less rather than more efficient.

But the practical size of airships seems to be limited only by the size of sheds big enough to build them in. At the same time the cost goes up pretty steeply, until it gets within shouting distance of the price of a battleship. This is one reason why the airships have seemed to move slowly into their place in the sun. A few thousand dollars can build an experimental plane, but it takes a few million to put an airship in the air so that somebody may find out what it is good for. If it turns out that some designer was a little too optimistic or the weather turns unreasonably nasty or something else occurs to spoil the experiment, it's a long and laborious job to find the money to try again.

At the same time, we need to recall that a lot of work has been done on lighter-than-air craft, and these new ships are by no means blind guesses or long chances. The first balloon went up not long after the Declaration of Independence, and something has been happening ever since. Germany built over a hundred Zeppelins before the war, carried 32,000 passengers in them, made a profit out of their operation, never had a passenger casualty in them nor lost one of them by structural failure in the air. The Goodyear Company,—which is now, as the Goodyear-Zeppelin Company, building America's two aerial giants,—has built a thousand balloons and over a hundred airships. This experience has not gone for nothing, nor have the few tragic failures of the bigger airships left behind no encouraging lessons for the future. Just as the modern plane has risen like a phoenix from the ashes of many sad crashes, so the future airship will owe much to the flights that failed.   And their principal lesson has been that airships must be big to be safe, just as they must be big to be useful.

So we cannot look just now for much in the way of sport-model airships, and the girls need not worry about walking home from balloon rides, at least in the immediate future. Further we can figure that the airship has a different job ahead of it than the airplane, and one which it is better suited for than the airplane can hope to be. This idea may irritate those heavier-than-air enthusiasts who claim that the airplane is good for anything, from cutting the grass to flagpole sitting, but it's a matter of business sense.   And if you examine closely into the present excitement over airships, you will find that a lot of it arises from the efforts of hard-headed business men to get in on a good thing.

Three nations are making bids for first honors in airship construction,—Germany, England and the United States.   Germany's program is a revival of the Zeppelin construction plan, with the considerable difference that it must get along now without much aid or comfort from government subsidy. Another big ship is planned to follow the trail of the *Graf*, but at present there is no hangar big enough to build it in. An experimental ship on a small scale was built this year, but it failed in trial flights, proving once again that little airships are not so good.   Whatever happens, however, to German airships in the near future, their construction will be principally for commercial purposes.

England got a nice share of the Zeppelins that were surrendered under the peace treaties and immediately made them

into floating laboratories of experiment or tore them apart
to see how they were done. There followed the construction
of the R.34, which made an elegant round trip to America, and
the R.38, which broke up principally because its designers
thought they might be able to cut corners a bit and build for
lightness and speed. The two five-million cubic-foot craft
that are now nearly ready for the air have an interesting idea
in back of them. England has a loose-jointed sort of empire,
spread in patches all over the round world, and now that the
colonies are becoming increasingly independent and self-suffi-
cient, it becomes increasingly important to keep them closely
in touch with the home office. The Secretary of State for Air
has preached for years the policy of encouraging air traffic
for the good it will do to empire efficiency. His program has
included airplane lines over land and airship lines across the
seas and the wide open spaces of desert and rough country
that make up the insides of some of the continents. He
wants to be able to call a meeting of the board of directors
of the British Empire, the premiers and governors of the
colonies, and have these gentlemen on hand in a few days
instead of a few weeks. There's no way to do it except
by air.

So the two big British ships will make their first long trips to
opposite ends of the empire. One will fly to Montreal, where a
mooring mast is ready. The other will set out for India, making
a stop-over at the mooring mast in Egypt and harboring at a
place called Karachi, which is somewhere on the Indian map.
The first intention is to show that it can be done. The second

is to establish empire communications on the modern scale. The third is to encourage commercial enterprise to do the same. It is an old tradition of English policy that "trade follows the flag." The new lines of trade will follow the trails of these flagships of the air.

In the American story there was the *Shenandoah* and there is the *Los Angeles*. You will recall that the latter was a peace-offering from Germany, built to replace the two Zeppelins which were awarded to this country by the peace settlement and which were destroyed by their crews in a last-minute flare of misguided patriotism. She came over here under her own power, and for five years has cruised the American skies with safety and distinction. Recently she inaugurated our Aviation Week by completing a thousand-mile jaunt, which is still quite a distance for any craft of land, sea or air. Throughout her career to date she has behaved as a good little airship should, and is a credit to the lighter-than-air idea.

The two new ships which will be assembled soon at Akron are for the Navy. They are warships of the air, with fighting planes in their insides and a mean disposition when roused. But behind and beyond them may be seen the shadow of future commercial craft, based on their experience and using the skill and machinery and equipment gathered from all over the world for their construction. Somebody had to build these first ships, and it's a perfectly good idea for the Navy to do it. The whole job won't cost as much as a single battleship, and the probable profits of the undertaking make a battleship look like a waste of time and money.

They represent a perfectly sound idea from a military point of view. They promise to be an essential link between surface craft which patrol the high seas and the coastwise defenses of fighting planes. Their effective range is three or four thousand miles and they can stay in the air away from their base of supplies for a week. They can survey three hundred square miles of sea at a time, and by radio communication direct the fleet below. They will be able to take care of themselves in any sort of weather short of hurricanes, and they can fly high and fast enough to ignore any enemy save the fighting plane. The development of the mooring mast has made them easy to handle in port, so that a score of men can tie them up and they can stay hitched to the mast for months at a time, using the big hangars only as dry docks.

But these facts are interesting chiefly because they justify what is in fact an expensive experiment. People are still prone to ask what such ships are good for in times of peace, even if they admit their usefulness in times of war. And there is no doubt that the Government in building them has its eye on commercial possibilities as much or more as on military usefulness. What, for instance, can you do with an airship that you can't do with any other craft designed by the fertile ingenuity of man?

As far as America's present program goes, the answer lies in the fact that there is a great deal more water in this world than anything else. The continents are patches on a water-logged globe, and there are big jumps between them. Two of these jumps are particularly interesting to America, one of them being the Atlantic and the other the Pacific. These are very handy water hazards against foreign interference with our own private peace and happiness, but they also slow up the more peaceable communications between nations on which the world's prosperity depends.

The first essential of any useful flying machine is that it shall have somewhere to go. These ships of the air, which don't give a hoot for highways and can travel 2,000 miles a day, can cross an ocean more quickly than anything save the airplane, and can do so more safely than the airplane because they need not come down if something breaks. Moreover, they can carry something beside fuel and a ham sandwich; they can carry a fair-sized crew, radio apparatus, a pay load of passengers and freight, and enough extra fuel to provide for emergencies, delays and detours. The best prospects for commercial airships lie across the seas, because they have definite and demonstrable advantages there over other means of locomotion. These, of course, are speed and comfort, which in these days are luxuries for which the traveler will pay cheerfully.

Of the two oceans that crowd our shores, the Atlantic is the more susceptible to bad weather, the narrower, and the one most traveled by crack liners. Moreover, the Atlantic is already a scene of airship competition between England and Germany, and there is not yet room for much more. But four thousand miles across the Pacific lies Hawaii, which is a place where all good Americans want to go to eat pineapples right from the pine trees and give the once-over to the hula maidens. The prospective airlines for American airships lie, therefore, over the Western sea, and unless all signs fail there will be airliners there within two years.

This is important not only to the people who want to float and run the lines, but to American prestige in the new phase of transportation. There's no use in blinking the fact that first come is first served when enterprise plays a new tune. We have lost advantage too often by moving slowly, to dare to ignore the prospects and promises of airship operation. Across the Pacific, at least, the first airship lines should be American lines.

The likelihood of quick inauguration of such service depends on two chief factors. The first is the success of these two ships at Akron, the second is the Government's willingness to turn over the transport of first-class mail to the airliners. The second depends to a considerable degree on the first. If airships can prove their reliability and stability and safety, their advantage of speed means much to the mail. Moreover, the Postoffice Department has been admirably willing to encourage air transportation by granting mail carrying to airlines wherever possible. With such an indirect subsidy from mail-carrying profits, passenger rates by airship can be brought down to the point where people will be ready to pay them.

In this program, America has very considerable advantages. In the first place, the craftsmen now building have the skill and experience of the Zeppelin builders behind them. The pick of the German shops are now on this side of the Atlantic, and there will be no such mistakes as wrecked more than one experimental ship in the past few years. Secondly, there is plenty of money here, and it takes money to build airships right. Third, there is business here, and a traveling public that is friendly to the new thing. Fourthly, there is helium, which is nature's most generous contribution to our airship program. The familiar advantages of helium are made more impressive by the disappointing delay to the *Graf's* attempt to cross the Atlantic for a second time. The new American ships, helium filled and safe from fire, will not only be more comfortable because heated and equipped with cooking facilities, smoking rooms and all the comforts of home, but will also carry all their essential arrangements within the hull, which is where they will be found in a ship of the sea. Nothing but the propellers stick out beyond the smooth outer jacket of these leviathans of the air. Engine trouble does not mean a precarious job of repair in a tiny gondola slung above thin air, but a comparatively safe and simple job within the ship itself. Since an airship underpowered is in danger of every breeze that blows, the ability to care for engines in flight is essential, and this the American ships will have to greater degree than any aircraft yet built.

It looks like the airships' turn. The bigger and better balloons are coming back into the picture, and it seems likely that America will have a large share in putting them there. Later on, it will be the public's job to keep them there, by giving them business so far as they deserve it. The public has well supported the airplane, and it's a fairly safe bet that the airliners will not lack customers when they are ready to fly.

FIELD LIGHTING, RADIO AND INTER-FIELD COMMUNICATIONS

BY F. C. HINGSBURG

Chief Engineer, Airways Division, U. S. Department of Commerce

THE United States has assumed leadership in the development of night flying and this is due primarily to the necessity of flying the mail at night. Each night more than 15,000 miles are flown over the airways in darkness, under all conditions of weather. The terminal fields and airports along the routes are under the management of municipalities and private enterprise.

Terminal airports with adequate lighting facilities for night landings are essential to insure that every landing will be a safe one. Bad weather, delayed schedules or a forced landing may cause delays, and airplanes may arrive at the airport at any time, night or day. At night the first concern of the pilot is to pick up the flash of the airport beacon that locates the terminal field. It is a comfortable feeling conducive to safety of operations to know that the lighting system at the airport is operated reliably from sunset to sunrise. A green auxiliary light flashing a distinctive code signal of 5,000 candlepower identifies the terminal field with positiveness. The airport beacon may be a flashing beacon of 100,000 candlepower with luminous period of 10 per cent or a 24-inch rotating beacon. The Department of Commerce rotating beacon has a 1000-watt airway lamp and 24-inch parabolic mirror developing a 2,000,000 candlepower flash which is shown every 10 seconds.   Prisms on the front cover glass

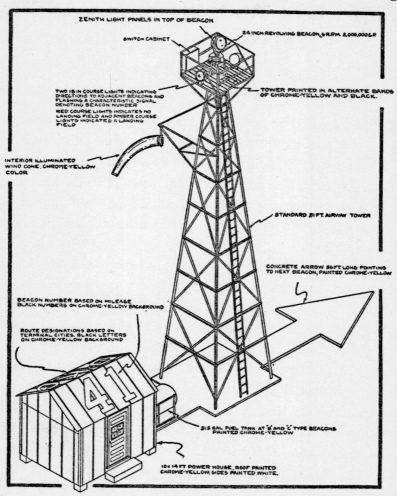

Standard Installation of Airways Beacon

deflect light upward from the horizon to plus 55 degrees, which provides the required light indication for airplanes at close range or flying at high altitudes. The zenith light is especially advantageous at landing fields. Under conditions of low ceiling, the zenith light plays on the clouds in an interesting manner as the airways beacons rotate and the pilot cannot fail to note the changing conditions of atmosphere as he passes over the airway. A lamp exchanger increases the reliability of the airport beacon. The beacon is motor-driven and an auxiliary contact mechanism synchronized with the period of revolution furnishes current to the course lights or the auxiliary green code light for airport identification. The airways beacons are mounted on structural steel towers, whereas airport beacons are usually mounted on the hangar roof and the light is elevated to project on an airplane 1000 feet above the adjacent beacon.

Having located the airport, the pilot maneuvers for position to land and his next concern is to learn the shape and extent of the landing area and best runways. The landing area is outlined with white or yellow boundary lights spaced approximately 250 feet apart around the field. Boundary cones are sometimes used in conjunction with the lighting system. Red obstruction lights are mounted on all obstructions surrounding the field. Where practicable the obstruction lights are in the boundary circuit. The principal runways are marked with green range lights. Multiple circuits are used for intermediate fields, whereas the series circuit is usually found advantageous for airports. Multiple circuits require the use of 25-watt, inside frosted lamps for white lights, but 50-watt lamps are used for colored lights to show up distinctly the same distance as the white lights. Series lighting requires 600 lumen 6.6 ampere lamp for white lights. In series lighting the open voltage above ground must be less than 450 volts and the operating voltage 310 volts. The details of the circuits are described in the Airport Rating Regulations. At Templehof, Berlin's noted airport, neon tube lights have been effectively used to border-light the landing area. This system is especially advantageous to contrast with competitive lights and the airport is unmistakably and distinctively marked. The neon lights have not been found to have fog-penetrating characteristics in this country, but the color characteristic has some advantages in the matter of visibility in thick weather.

All landings are made into the wind, and for this purpose the wind direction must be observed from the lighted wind tee or wind cone. Neon or mercury-argon lights are very effective for outlining the wind tee. The wind indicator should be visible at least 1000 feet and show the true direction of the wind. The hangars and other buildings are flood-lighted for perspective indication by use of industrial reflectors or flood-light projectors, the average illumination being 2½-foot candles.

In making landing at intermediate fields, the pilot uses the wing tip flood-lights mounted on the airplane, and for night flying all airplanes should be so equipped. In addition the airplanes should carry parachute flares to be dropped in the event of a forced emergency landing due to motor failure or other causes, in order that a suitable landing place may be selected by the pilot and the best possible emergency landing made. Fortunately these landings are infrequent, and largely avoidable when adequately powered multi-motored airplanes are used.

At airports, however, a landing field flood-lighting system should be provided that will illuminate the landing area to a minimum vertical plane intensity of not less than 0.15 foot

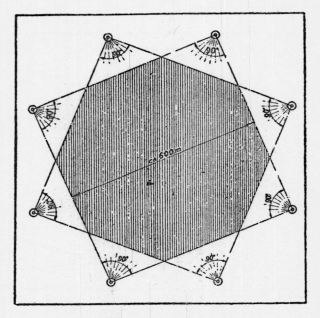

Flood-lighting System Used in Europe

candles. There are two methods of installing flood-lights at airports. The centralized system has the flood-lights grouped in one location. The distributed system uses flood-light units spaced about 250 feet apart along the sides of the airport.

The European practice is to use the distributed system with flood-lights mounted close to the ground and illuminating the entire landing area. The advantage claimed is reduction of shadows by directing the light from several sources. The same practice is followed for irregular shaped fields. The glare is eliminated by sharp cut-off using especially designed lamps with small filament heights. Five hundred M.M. dioptric lenses with 3 kilowatt lamps are used.

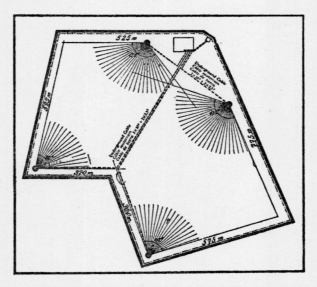

Illuminating an Unsystematical Field

The usual practice in the United States is to group the lights at one point or along one or more sides in such a manner as to permit the pilot to look out one side of the cockpit in landing without facing the flood-lights.

This system concentrates all the glare in one location and the

pilot is careful not to look into the light source when he is making
a landing. Two types of flood-lighting equipment are used for
landing field lights, the dioptric lens system and the reflector
system. The dioptric lens system is made in three sizes, 1000
M.M. diameter, using the high intensity arc or 10 kilowatt

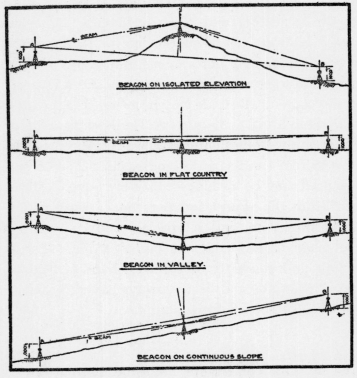

Method of Setting Axes of Acetylene Route Beacons

incandescent lamp for centralized installation; 500 M.M.
diameter lens for the grouped or distributed system, using at
least two units with 10 kilowatt lamps, and small 200 or 300 M.M.

units installed along the boundary of the landing area about 250 feet apart and using 1500-watt lamps.   There are several types of equipment designed on the reflector system.   A common type is the 24-inch parabolic unit with 3 kilowatt incandescent lamps and used for either the centralized or distributed system. Another type is the twin airport flood-light, using 2 to 10 kilowatt lamps in two reflectors, and the parabolinear light having a number of 3 kilowatt lamps in the line of focal points.   The parabocylindric flood-light units are made in sizes to accommodate 5 kilowatt, 3 kilowatt and 1500-watt lamps and are used for the distributed system, or the units may be grouped in the centralized system of flood-lighting.   About 15 to 24 kilowatts are required to produce the required minimum vertical plane intensity of illumination of 0.15 foot candles on a landing field 2,500 feet square. The lamps used may be incandescent or arc lamps.   The system to be installed at the airport and the type of apparatus depends upon local conditions, and a special study of each airport should be made to arrive at the best solution.   The color of ground, slope and character of surface, shape of field, obstructions, prevailing winds and best runways have a bearing on the proper selection of flood-lighting equipment.

RADIO DIRECTION

Airways lighting consists of rotating beacons and course lights spaced 10 miles apart along the route with lighted intermediate fields at 30-mile spacing.   As much as the pilot appreciates this remarkable system of lighting, it is ineffective in fog. The moment the coolness of a cloud bank enfolds him, he is blind and lost unless some unseen hand is stretched forth to guide him.   In a rolling sea of blinding vapor, radio direction keeps him on his course.   The antenna system of the radio beacon consists of two directional loops supported on a pole. In the small building at the foot of the pole a transmitter is located.   It transmits a characteristic signal from equivalent loops alternately in a character that interlocks, marking a radio course by interlocking dashes.   There are four courses, each approximately three degrees in width, rang-

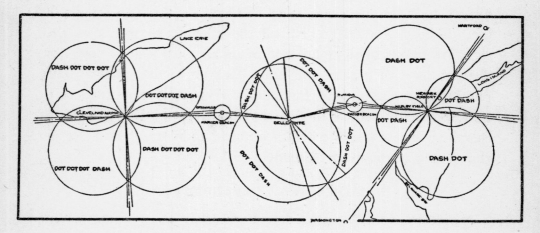

Diagram Showing Operating Range of Beacons on New York-Cleveland Course

ing from the radio beacon, and these can be shifted by means of the goniometer to coincide with the lighted airway.   A simple receiver with ear-phones fitted in the helmet enables the pilot to hear the aural signal from the beacon.

The conventional pattern of the directional radio beacon range is used at Cleveland to mark east and west courses of the Transcontinental from Cleveland.   At Bellefonte the pattern has been warped by use of a vertical antenna in conjunction with each directional loop and the radio course is bent at the beacon to mark the axis of the lighted airway.   At Hadley Field, the strength of the signal from one of the loops was cut down by resistance and the pattern and interlock altered to radio-mark the courses leading to Washington and Hartford in addition to the Transcontinental Airway.

The pilot follows the radio-marked course over the lighted airway and is on his course when he hears a continuous stream of long dashes.   Should he drift off the course, the pilot loses the signal from one of the loops and hears the dot-dash or dash-dot characteristic of beacon and pulls back on to the course.   The pilot is thus enabled to fly blindly through the storm-tossed atmosphere high above the fog-enveloped earth if he knows with certainty that a definite distance ahead there are clear skies or that a safe landing can be made.

WEATHER AND COMMUNICATIONS

A system of broadcasting hourly weather and landing conditions at principal fields along the route has been started on the Transcontinental between Cleveland and New York.   Caretakers at the intermediate fields and the airports along the route transmit reports on the teletype system each hour, and this data is broadcast, followed by the Weather Bureau digest of conditions along the route.   This system is being extended to San Francisco and to other airways as soon as the Airways Radio Stations can be completed.   The radio broadcast reports make it possible for the pilot to be kept advised as to changing weather and landing conditions along the route and at his terminal airport. Other messages necessary for the safety of airplanes in flight will be transmitted from the chain of Airways Radio Stations.

The Weather Bureau is the responsible agency for interpreting weather reports and making weather forecasts, but substantial co-operative assistance can be rendered to provide the timely weather information required for flying. Data collected at airports is most valuable. A limited appropriation available July 1, 1929, makes it possible to provide, for the first time in the United States, adequate weather service gathered every three hours through a secondary net system. The weather data for the secondary net is telegraphed to Weather Bureau control centers, where weather maps are prepared and forecasts covering the geographic area made, and transmitted over the Department of Commerce communications system and broadcast by the Airways Radio Stations. All airports within several miles of any Airways Radio Station may tune in on the station and receive weather forecasts, visibility and ceiling height information for all points in their geographic area.

To be included in the secondary net reports may be considered an exceptional opportunity by any airport, since the data furnished is made available to all other airports in the geographical area by the radio broadcast system. The operations manager of the airport may, under this plan, be appointed special weather bureau representative at one dollar per year and the messages will be sent by telegraph at Government rates. Reports from about 200 to 300 airports in the United States are required in the three-hour secondary net system to prepare proper forecasts. In addition, reports will also be required from other airports covering ceiling and visibility data when landing conditions are hazardous. This data will be broadcast from the Airways Radio Stations each hour. Pilots in flight and all other airports in the geographic area will receive the radio broadcast of weather and landing conditions. This is an inexpensive method of participating in a system of adequate weather information for safe flying. Areas of fog and storm may be fully charted from the data submitted and the weather hazards taken out of air transportation.

The telegraph companies have promised full co-operation in the handling of fast communications from airports. The restricted radio spectrum does not permit the establishment of airport radio stations for point and inter-field communications, and land lines must be used.

Communications with airplanes in flight can only be accomplished by radio and in the future all landing and take-off orders will be given by the operations manager of the airport by radio. An exclusive frequency will be set up for this purpose and all pilots will be required to tune in on this frequency when landing, taxiing on the field or taking off from the airport. The airport transmitter will be of low power and range so regulated as not to interfere with other airports.

In addition to weather reports, the Department of Commerce will broadcast each hour such messages to airplanes in flight as may be found necessary for safety of flight. The ground stations of the Department of Commerce will stand a watch, on the assigned calling and distress frequency, for emergency calls from airplanes in flight. Where the communication service rendered by the Department of Commerce is inadequate or non-existent, air transport companies may establish radio stations in which all companies may participate, sharing equal service, costs and liability. Exclusive radio frequencies will be assigned to established civil airways, on which this radio service will operate, to communicate with airplanes in flight. This service is not available for point to point communications.

Any airplane equipped with a simple receiver will be able to receive radio direction, weather broadcasts, emergency messages and airport landing directions. A wind-driven generator makes it unnecessary to carry "A" and "B" batteries aboard the plane, but on the other hand, the set cannot function when on the ground. Future regulations will require all airplanes carrying passengers in interstate traffic to have a receiving set in proper operating condition. Airplanes carrying more than six persons will be required by regulations to carry a radio transmitter for emergency communications over the route. Under the present policy, airplanes with radio transmitters may communicate with the air transport companies' radio stations when flying an established route, and when approaching or flying over an airport may communicate at close range with the airport manager on the exclusive frequency set up for this purpose.

This system when fully established overcomes the present great obstacle to commercial efficiency of aviation. It will never be possible to turn aside the destructive onslaughts of storms, nor will we be likely to dissolve the blinding fog, but every airport and airplane within the reach of the Airways Radio network may know every hour what weather conditions are at all points of the compass and at any distance beyond the immediate horizon. Accurate knowledge of conditions and an efficient communications system for disseminating this information are the guiding spirits that bring the pilot safely through.

SOARING FLIGHTS AT CAPE COD

BY DANIEL ROCHFORD

I RAN as fast as I could; fell over the edge of a cliff; somebody came falling over me, giving me a kick in the ear as he went past; then five more men came hurtling through the air on to me, pushing my face down the side of the sand mountain as though I were a baseball player sliding for home. Then I jumped up with my mouth full of sand and cheered madly.

For high above me sailed the *Professor*, prize soaring plane of the AMAC Cape Cod Glider School, making its first flight in America. I had been lead man on the right-hand rubber launching rope. The start had been made from the sand bluffs at Corn Hill on the Massachusetts Bay side of Cape Cod where Peter Hesselbach a year ago made the record of four hours five minutes soaring in the *Darmstadt*. So short is the running place there that we had to jump right over the edge and down the side toward the beach 125 feet below. But we didn't mind. For Rolf von Chlingensperg, sent over with Heinrich Knott by the Rhoen-Rossitten Gesellschaft to instruct Americans in gliding and soaring, was riding the upwind, coasting with his nose out toward the bay, riding along the up-flowing air pouring up the cliffs from the sea.

That was the fourth of August. "Clingey" flew for fifteen minutes. He had flown back over the launching place and was about to turn where the sand cliffs slope down to an inlet. The wind slackened as he turned. He swung the plane directly into the wind and slid clear across the inlet to an exposed sand dune on the other side. He made a beautiful landing.

I had gotten my camera and gone down to the beach. The rest of the crowd was still up top. I rejoined them. Knott, who is chief instructor and had let Chlingensperg make the first flight, looked gloomy. We followed his gaze. There was a city block of open water between our shore and the place where the *Professor* had just landed.

But we got bathing suits and a rowboat and went after the sailplane. We loaded its nose into the rowboat and forded the inlet. Volunteers from among the spectators were collected. We hooked a rope on to the nose of the sailplane and hauled it right up the face of the bank. It was reversed and placed into the wind. Knott, still in his wet bathing suit, climbed into the cockpit. The boys formed to handle the rubber catapulting ropes. I rubbed my ear and pretended to be very busy taking photographs.

"Pool oudt!" shouted Knott. The seven men on each rope walked forward. "Grrun!" shouted Knott. They raced for the cliff. But the wind had stiffened to twenty-five miles an hour. As the rubber ropes tautened and began to sing, "Clingey" let go the tail. Knott climbed as steeply as ever a slotted winged airplane climbs. Then he slid, quartering the wind, along the cliff. Over a high place he turned into the wind. Almost motionless he hovered, pointed into the teeth of the breeze. Even as we watched he lifted above us. Higher and higher until he had almost 300 feet over the heights of the dunes.

Then off down the shore, a quarter mile, a half mile, a mile. Almost lost, a speck in the distance. Finally he turned. The sun flashed back from his wing topside as he dipped for the turn. Then back over us. Ten minutes went to twenty; twenty to thirty; thirty to forty. Finally after three-quarters of an hour he came again overhead. "I'm landing," he shouted. On over the cottages to the end of the bluff. An easy turn. A nervous instant, then, as the wind seemed certain to brush him back on to the hillside. He slipped the plane magnificently, down and out on to the airstream. Then nose down he coasted for some sand flats. The tide had been going out and nature had made a runaway out ahead of him, right into the wind. Down over it he skimmed, drifting to a perfect landing beyond.

He was shivering and blue when we reached him. His eyes were watering as though he had hay fever. We did not have to ask him why he had landed. The wind held until dark. He could have gone on that day to a new American record. He didn't. I wonder if flying records have ever before been merely a matter of woolen underwear and goggles?

Several of the American students wanted to take a crack at the *Professor*. But they hadn't qualified yet for their soaring ratings with the Pruefling school soaring planes and were refused.

Since those first flights, the school has had its Prueflings in the air many days. From the sand bluffs on the Atlantic Ocean side where the school is built, the students have sailed out over

the sea, turning on to the beach.   That last turn is not without
its risks.   The first student to land himself in the ocean was
George O. Smith of New York, aged 19.   He began his turn too
late and nosed into about seven feet of sea.   Excitement prevailed and even Major Clarence Doll, school commandant,
rushed in with his clothes on to aid the rescue.   Smith unfastened
his safety belt before he hit and was only the worse by a ducking.

The first student to win the primary rating was John Perkins
of Connecticut, a power plane pilot.   The three ratings are
based exactly on the German system: i.e., thirty seconds simple
glide for the basic; one-minute glide, with left and right hand
turns, for the secondary; and a five-minute soaring flight for the
advanced rating.   When you win all three ratings you are
issued a license.   But not until then.   For, as General Manager
Vergne Chappelle of the AMAC says, "There is no third or two-
thirds about it.   We give a license when you are qualified to
pilot.   Talk about licensing a flier who has merely made a
glide, or a glide with turns, is like giving an auto driver a license
for driving straight ahead, another when he can back up or turn
around, and a third when he is fit to handle a car."

Whatever the glider events at the National Air Races may or
may not show, the developing of the sailplane sport in America
demands centers for soaring flight.   Gliding is good fun at first.
But it becomes monotonous.   The tendency is to try to get
thrills by stunts.

Towing sailplanes behind power planes is naturally a trick
only for qualified pilots.   Wallace H. Franklin of Michigan has
done this very successfully.   Knott and Chlingensperg on Cape

Cod plan a series of such flights in order to place their soaring plane beneath cumulous clouds. Then they will cut free and try to remain aloft by getting from one cloud to another.

The lifting currents are strongest just at the base of such a cloud. I have noticed countless times, when flying power planes up through cloud formations, that the clouds all seem to be as level at the base as though somebody had taken a knife and cut them off.

The very fact that the cloud is there proves that there is an up-wind. In fact, the cloud sits right on the top of the column of rising air.

Towing sailplanes behind airplanes was also done by Dale Drake in California early this year. Perhaps the most impressive example of this will probably have been shown to the American public by the time these lines are in print. I have talked with the German "air train" experts who came to this country last month and whose presence was kept a secret. They trail two sailplanes and then cut loose and perform all manner of antics.

Such uses of sailplanes are for the experts. Soaring under proper conditions offers thrills enough for the beginner. But soaring centers are not numerous. Germany has now three great centers at the schools on the Wasserkuppe mountain near Frankfort, on the Rossitten sand dunes beyond Konigsberg in East Prussia, and on the Riesen mountains of Silesia near Grunau. The last-named school has only recently attracted international notice. It started with local sailplane club activities in 1924 and this year has begun to rival the other two schools. I was able to win my one-bird rating at Rossitten, although I was there only one day this spring. The terrain is more favorable.

But Paul Roehre, commandant of the Rossitten school and the 1928 head of the AMAC Cape Cod Glider Camp at which Blunk earned his bird, told me that to win two birds at Rossitten a student must soar. The sinking speed, as they call gliding angle for sailplanes, is such that the student could not possibly take a full minute to get from the top of the dunes to the bottom. He must ride the winds to delay his descent. Of course the five-minute flight is genuine soaring.

The mountain school at the Wasserkuppe, from which the two Cape Cod instructors this year came, is better as far as making the first two ratings are concerned, because the mountain is high enough, as I found out when I climbed it in an April snowstorm this year, to permit of several minutes' straightway gliding. The difficulty there is with the landing, because of rocks on the slopes and trees and brush.

It is wonderful that the National Glider Association was formed and is working so generally for the spread of the sport. It is fine that several manufacturers have now taken up making sailplanes. It is most helpful that the colleges with aeronautical laboratories are getting interested in problems of sailplane design and improvement.

But the whole development of the sport, and its greater service to aviation as a step toward power plane piloting, demands several good soaring centers and schools for advanced study and for the teaching of sailplane instructors who can return to the individual clubs and communities and be responsible for activities there.

Donald Walker of the N.G.A. visited the Cape school last month and was impressed with the new steel hangars, the dozen sailplanes of different types, the terrain, and the general organization of the camp. He believes the school will become one of the great advanced sailplane training centers.

My own personal experience on Cape Cod has been that the other side of the Cape is better for soaring in the summer season. That was what Roehre said. The prevailing winds give soaring velocities much more regularly from the bay side than from the bluffs where the school now is.

But the Corn Hill site, as may be gathered from the introduction to this article, is not a place for beginners.

The AMAC expects to build a hangar at Corn Hill for storing a few soaring planes. Qualified students will be allowed to fly from there. Preliminary student soaring will have to be done from the Atlantic Ocean side by the school buildings. At present the *Professor* has to be hauled across the Cape on a truck or trailer when wind conditions indicate good soaring on the other side. The *Professor* can be taken apart in a half hour or less. But the Pruefling student soaring planes cannot be disassembled so readily and hence cannot be hauled back and forth.

I believe another year will see a soaring school in the South, perhaps near famous Kitty Hawk in Carolina; one in California; one in the state of Washington; and one in the Middle West. Last year on a flight to Minnesota, I recall a lot of sand dunes with sand blown clear inshore along Lake Michigan's southern bounds.   A school in that section would be most beneficial.

For soaring, the real need is for mountains or high sand dunes by water where there are plenty of good strong winds blowing on to the shore.   And without soaring, the American sailplane sport and business will be like the young lady who was all dressed up but had no place to go.

ACKNOWLEDGMENTS

The Editor and Publishers deeply appreciate the co-operation and assistance rendered by the following publications in granting permission to use the material printed in this book. They doubly appreciate this assistance inasmuch as they feel that all concerned are making a definite contribution to the interest of Youth in aerial progress:

AERO DIGEST.

> *My Flight to 39,140 Feet.*
> *The Yardsticker Sailplane.*
> *Some Recent Spectacular Flights.*
> *Around the World by Airship.*
> *Parachutes!*
> *European Flying Impressions.*
> *Present Status of Commercial Aeronautics in Europe.*
> *Greatest of All Sports.*
> *Passing of Pioneer Days.*
> *Training a Thousand Air Students.*
> *Life of a Flying Cadet.*
> *Air Patrol of the Coast Guard.*
> *Commercial Aviation in the Yukon.*
> *The Flying General.*
> *Flight of Williams and Yancey.*
> *Flaming Gas Beacons?*
> *Pegasus, "The Flying Horse."*
> *Bigger and Better Balloons.*
> *Field Lighting, Radio, and Inter-Field Communications.*
> *Soaring Flights at Cape Cod.*

315

AERONAUTICAL PUBLICATIONS, INC.

Two Tough Hombres.
The Monster Dornier Do.X.
A Pilot's Wife Speaking.
Learning to Fly Commercially.
Army Flight Training.
Where Does Congress Stand?
Twenty Feet in the Air.

CANADIAN AIR REVIEW.

Canada Honors First Atlantic Flyers.
Aerial Post Offices Now Practical.
Wireless for Light Aeroplanes.
The Story of Flight.
Never Has Been Airplane Engine.
Safety in the Air.

THE NEW YORK TIMES.

America from a Skimming Plane.
Flirting with Death in a Parachute!
Women Find Place Among Fliers.

NEW YORK AMERICAN WEEKLY.

Before Everybody Can Fly.